Thai Cookbook

Learn How to Prepare Traditional and Modern Thai Comfort Food at Home, Cooking Over 100 Dishes Plus Vegetarian and Spicy Slow Cooker Recipes

By

Adele Tyler

All trademarks and brands within this book are for clarifying purposes only and are owned by the owners themselves, not affiliated with this document.

Table of contents

CHAPTER 7: THAI VEGETARIAN AND SLOW COOKER RECIPES 115

Introduction

Food is an integral part of our daily routine. Without the intake of healthy, nutritious, and tasty food, life can really turn into a challenge. Often, cooking is considered a tough job due to lack of our knowledge and skills regarding it. But it is the other way round, once you start getting familiar with the skill of cooking. Cooking is an art, and you can also be an artist if you start cooking food at your home.

This book is majorly about Thai cuisine. Thai food is the public cooking of Thailand. Thai cooking places accentuation on light meals with amazing aromatic segments and a spicy or zesty edge. Thai cooking is about the shuffling of different components to make an amicable completion. Like an unpredictable melodic harmony, it must have a smooth surface, yet it does not make a difference what is going on underneath. Simplicity is not the proclamation here, by any means.

In this cookbook, you will learn the history and origin of Thai food as well as the history of traditional Thai dishes. You are going to get all the information regarding the evolution of Thai cuisine over the years. You will get to know the reasons behind the popularity of Thai food across the U.S.A.

You will always be finding yourself at ease while cooking Thai food at home, and find exactly why cooking Thai food at home is way better than any Dine-in experience.

There are various health benefits of having Thai food at home, and you will learn all of these benefits when you go through the different properties of spices used in Thai foods. You will get over 100 different breakfast, lunch, dinner, and dessert, famous, alternative, vegetarian, and slow cooker recipes that you can easily start cooking at home with the detailed instructions present below each recipe.

Preparing your Thai food at home without the need to order food from some restaurant can become very easy once you start reading this book. So, why wait for more? Let us dive deep into the world of Thai cuisine.

Chapter 1: Introduction to Thai Food

Thailand is the most acclaimed nation in the whole world for its cooking. Traversing from the southern landmass toward the northern regions, the nation offers a various mix of madly flavorful food.

The south of Thailand is acclaimed for its fiery curries, weighty utilization of coconut milk, and amazing fish recipes. The northeastern part is notable for its veggie filled plates of mixed greens and spices, barbecued meat, hotdogs, and clingy rice. Bangkok, the biggest city, draws in Thais from all around the nation to make an endless blend of enticing flavors to taste.

From streak cooked sautés to hand beaten servings of mixed greens, if you appreciate eating, you will be in heaven with the assortment and amount of food in this cuisine.

1.1 History and Origin of Thai Food

Thai food began with the individuals who emigrated from the southern Chinese territories to cutting edge Thailand, hundreds of years back. Truly there were multiple Szechwan impacts in Thai cooking; however, throughout the long term, numerous different impacts have influenced Thai food.

In the past, Buddhist priests brought an Indian touch to the food, and southern Muslim states affected the cooking in the south of Thailand. A lot later, Thai food was impacted by European cuisine after contact with Portuguese ministers and Dutch brokers. During these occasions, there was some impact from the Japanese.

Thailand is a major nation with an assorted topography, and throughout the long term, this has prompted the improvement of local divergences in its style of foods.

1.2 History of Traditional Thai Dishes

Thai food was customarily eaten while sitting on mats or covers on the floor; these customs actually are still found in the more traditional family units. Currently, there are four distinct styles of cooking in Traditional Thai cuisine:

- Southern Thai cooking is the most mainstream outside of Thailand since that is the primary traveler area of the nation. In southern cooking, there is considerably more utilization of coconut milk in numerous dishes. Coconut replaces Ghee for fricasseeing, and there is a substantial utilization of fish in the dishes.

- The food in the north east is impacted by Laos; when in doubt, the food is exceptionally spiced, and clingy glutinous rice is the favored staple for north-eastern dishes. Despite the fact that there are a lot of meat dishes, generally, meat was scant in the towns, and the principle wellspring of protein were shrimp and freshwater fish.

- The central area offers food that is halfway between the north and south; however, fragrant Jasmine rice is preferred by many to the clingy assortment. What makes the focal area food unique is that it is home to illustrious cooking.

- The cooking in northern Thailand is commonly milder than in the remainder of the nation; clingy rice is preferred, customarily it is massaged into little balls with the fingers.

1.3 Evolution of Thai Food over Time

Traditionally, Thai cooking sets aside a great deal of effort to plan. Consequently, planning food requires loads of participation and cooperation, including the relatives to cook it all together as a feast. The food clarifies the Thai life and its conventions, customs, and culture. Thai families are huge and well-weave. In cooking, Thai relatives help each other as a group. In cooking curries, youngsters help with light work like nipping off basil leaves, and grown-ups press coconut meat and pound chilies and flavors.

In the present day, making Thai food is a lot simpler as all the things are promptly accessible in general stores, yet there is an analysis that it does not have the customary standards of the past.

1.4 Popularity of Thai Dishes in the U.S.A

Thai food is not the only cuisine to have been changed in the excursion across seas. Various eateries in the USA serve dishes that regard the intricacy of Thai food and its equalization of sweet, sharp, salt, and zest. They are important for an ocean change that, as of late, has delivered amazing and acclaimed Thai cafés around the entire nation.

Eateries serving great Thai food, as they do now, did not exist twenty years before because there was no network to help it grow.

Utilizing a strategy currently known as gastro diplomacy or culinary discretion, the legislature of Thailand has purposefully supported the presence of Thai cooking outside of Thailand to build its fare and the travel industry incomes, just as its noticeable quality on the social and conciliatory stages.

The techniques for accomplishing this expansion were complex, run in equal by different divisions of the legislature. The Ministry of Commerce's Department of Export Promotion, in all probability run by officials as opposed to restaurateurs, drew up models for three diverse "Ace Eateries," which financial specialists could pick as such a pre-assembled eatery plan, from stylish to menu contributions.

Since huge business sectors like the United States have been immovably settled as admirers of coconut milk and nut sauce, the Thai government has been making a push to expand the presence of Thai cooking in new areas, particularly the Middle East.

Chapter 2: Thai Food: Home Cooking Vs. Dine- in Experience

Individuals all around the globe are occupied. Everyone is either occupied with work, school or other additional daily activities. Nobody actually has the opportunity to cook, so families are continually going out to eat at any preferred eatery. In this chapter we will discuss the difference between eating at home and eating at an eatery as far as the value, tidiness, taste and administration are concerned.

2.1 Difference between Home Cooking Vs. Dine-in Experience

With applications that permit you to arrange with simply a couple of taps, it tends to be incredibly enticing to swear off preparing supper at home. Yet, there are frequently compromises for comfort. Café suppers can contain loads of unhealthy substances.

There is additionally a great deal past what is in the supper that you pass up when you are eating from a take-away meal box. Following are the differences between home cooking and dine-in experience:

1. Healthy Food

Some research studies propose that individuals more frequently, instead of getting a take-out meal, have a generally more beneficial eating regimen. These examinations additionally show that café suppers ordinarily contain higher measures of sodium, immersed fat, absolute fat, and large number of calories than home-prepared dinners. While by cooking yourself at home, you have all the authority over what is going in your food. That can improve things significantly to your general wellbeing.

2. More Family Time

Cooking together can offer you an occasion to reconnect with your accomplice as well as friends and family. Cooking has different advantages too. The American Psychological Association expresses that trying new things together like learning another recipe together can help keep a couple associated and occupied with their relationship.

3. Save Plenty of Time

Part of ordering take-out means waiting for the food to arrive or driving to get it. Depending on where you live, what time you order, and whether or not the delivery person is good with directions, this could actually take more time than if you would simply make a meal at home.

Cooking at home does not have to take a lot of time if you do not want it to.

By using different services, you eliminate the need to look for recipes or grocery shop. Everything you need comes right to your door; in the exact pre-portioned amounts you will be using.

4. Save Money

In the long run, preparing meals at home may save you money. A group of basic ingredients often comes in at a lower price tag than a single restaurant dish. You can also end up getting more meals out of a recipe you make at home than if you order takeout, or have leftovers to take to work the next day. After just a few weeks, you could see noticeable savings start to pile up.

5. It is Fun

When you are making a meal from scratch, you get to discover and experiment with different ingredients, seasonings, and cuisines. And as with any activity, the more time you spend in the kitchen, the better you become at creating fantastic meals. You would be missing out this fun if you would keep on ordering your food or going for dine-in to any restaurant.

6. Personalization

Cooking at home gives you the opportunity to eat the foods you love exactly how you enjoy eating them. While, going for dine-in you would have to consume the food however it is prepared.

7. Maintain Calorie Count

The average fast-food order ranges between 1,100 to 1,200 calories total that is almost all of a woman's recommended daily calorie intake (1,600 to 2,400 calories) and almost two thirds of a man's daily intake (2,000 to 3,000 calories). And if you think independent restaurants and smaller chains do any better, think again.

Those eateries pump in even more calories, with an average of 1,327 calories per meal. Making a meal yourself means you can make sure the portion sizes and calorie counts are where you want them to be. Recipes often come with nutritional information and serving size suggestions, which makes that even easier.

So, it is better to cook home and eat healthy rather than heading off to a restaurant just due to your lazy routine.

2.2 Health Benefits of Thai Food

Thai food is ordinarily loved in the United States; however, you may puzzle over whether this cooking is healthy or not. The conventional eating routine of Thailand highlights vivid vegetables, fish, and meats that are presented with rice or noodles and prepared with spices and flavors like turmeric, galangal, Thai basil, and lemongrass. Food served at Western Thai eateries shares numerous parts of valid Thai cooking, despite the fact that it has some striking contrasts.

Thai menus in America may have bigger segments, more seared nourishments, and recipes that are higher in salt and sugar. Following are the health benefits of Thai food:

- Several of the most common Thai ingredients are nutritious on their own, but there are other healthy aspects of Thai food in general. For one, Thai meals often feature a good balance of macronutrients such as protein, fats, and carbs.

- Curries, stir-fries, and soups are made with a variety of vegetables, include a protein source like tofu, lean meat, or seafood, and contain coconut milk, peanut sauces, or other fat.

- The most commonly used veggies in Thai meals are non-starchy, such as peppers, tomato, cabbage, broccoli, carrots, and onions. These veggies are loaded with fiber, vitamins, minerals, and a variety of compounds that contribute to good digestion and overall health.

- Eating meals that largely comprise on non-starchy veggies and also contain protein and fat can help you maintain stable blood sugar levels throughout the day. This, in turn, leads to sustained energy and may aid weight loss.

Thai cuisine is known for incorporating regional herbs and spices, fresh vegetables, and lean proteins that add both flavor and nutrition to meals. However, some Westernized Thai dishes are deep fried, served in large portions, or contain excessive amounts of added sugar and salt. To choose a healthy Thai meal, opt for the dishes that are loaded with plant foods, contain a protein source, and feature a variety of herbs and spices.

2.3 Different Properties of Spices used in Thai Food

A large portion of the ingredients found in Thai food are a clear reflection of the environment that is warm with fertile land and abundant water. Recipes depend on fish, peculiar products of the soil, a few sorts of noodles and sauces.

Rice is the pillar of most dinners, giving an ideal similarity to the wide assortment of tastes and colors that encompass it. Hot flavoring mixes are utilized to season everything from the day's catch to the easy to make servings of rice or noodles.

Following are some of the main seasonings used in Thai cooking:

- **Cinnamon:** Thai cooks favor Chinese cinnamon, or Cinnamomum cassia, which is better, somewhat spicier, and more exceptional in color and flavor than Cinnamomum zeylanicum. Cinnamon's fragrance and flavor add to both sweet and exquisite Thai dishes, just as zest mixes.

- **Cumin:** Thai cooks roast aromatic, earthy cumin seed in a dry pan to bring out its flavor, and then grind it for use in curry pastes and other spice blends. Cumin is also a primary ingredient in many spice blends, soups, stews, and meat, bean and rice dishes.

- **Cilantro:** Also known as Chinese parsley, Thais use this soft, leafy plant for its distinctive flavor and earthy or musty aroma.

- **Basil:** Basil is used both as a flavoring and a garnish in Thai cooking, and handfuls are sometimes tossed into soups, curries and stir fries just before serving.

- **Cardamom:** The fragrant cardamom seedpod is used in the whole form in a few Thai dishes of Indian origin, like Mussamun Curry. A bit lemony, cardamom also has a slightly peppery and sweet taste and scent. Thai cooks often combine cardamom with other aromatic spices, like cinnamon, nutmeg, and mace.

- **Garlic:** Thai cooks value garlic for its health properties, aroma, and the fact that its flavor blends well with a variety of other spices. Garlic is a main ingredient in the traditional Big Four Seasonings Blend, along with salt, cilantro root, and white peppercorns.

- **Curry Powders and Pastes:** Thais commonly blend their own curry powders and pastes by grinding various herbs and spices in a mortar and pestle. Curries are used to flavor coconut milk, salad dressings, noodle sauces, seafood and meat dishes, vegetable dishes and soups.

- **Lemongrass:** The fresh, light, lemony flavor and scent of lemongrass is a staple in Thai cuisine. Thai cooks use the bulb and base leaves of lemongrass to season sauces, soups, stir-fries and curries. It enhances meats, poultry, seafood, and vegetables, and it's especially delicious with garlic, chilies and cilantro.

- **Nutmeg:** Thai cooks appreciate the intense aroma and sweet, spicy flavor of nutmeg in recipes for sweet and savory dishes. They use a grater to finely powder the whole spice.

- **Turmeric:** The robes of Buddhist monks in Thailand are colored with an ancient yellow dye made from turmeric. Its flavor is sweet, warm, and a little peppery, but it is used primarily for color in many Thai dishes, including curries, condiments, and seafood and grain dishes.

- **Cloves:** This dark brown, aromatic spice is used whole in the Thai kitchen. Its taste is distinct, sharp, and warm or sweet, and you will find it in both sweet and savory recipes.

- **Chili peppers:** Thai food is hot, thanks to its liberal use of fresh and dried chili peppers. Although chili peppers are not native, they are now essential to Thai cuisine.

- **Coriander:** The intensely aromatic and slightly piquant flavor of coriander seeds is prized in Thai cooking. Thai cooks often roast and then pound the seeds to release the flavor; they also use the root and the leaf (cilantro) of the plant.

- **Galangal:** A relative of ginger, this pale-yellow spice has a sharp, lemony, peppery hot taste. It is also known as galingale, Java root, or Siamese ginger. Large, thin pieces of galangal are used to flavor Thai soups, stews and curries; for pastes it is finely chopped and pounded. Ginger may be substituted for galangal in most of the Thai recipes.

- **Mace:** The sweet scent of "closed blossom," as the Thai cooks refer to mace, is enjoyed in dishes that have been influenced by Indian and Indonesian cookery. It is mildly nutty, warm taste is found in soups, stuffing, sauces and baked goods. It complements seafood, meats, and cheese, as well as some beverages.

Thai cuisine will appeal to any cook who loves the art of seasoning. And while many dishes are very hot, those prepared at home can be adjusted to just the right degree for your own tastes.

Chapter 3: The World of Thai Breakfast Recipes

Food is enormously significant in Thai culture, with Thais utilizing food as a typical friendly exchange. There are numerous well-known dishes in Thailand and a lot of territorial specialties. Following are some amazing breakfast recipes that you can easily make at home:

3.1 Thai Breakfast Omelette Recipe

Cooking Time: 15 minutes

Serving Size: 2

Ingredients:

- Vegetable oil, one and a half tbsp.

- Sliced mushrooms, one cup

- Eggs, eight

- Sliced red capsicum, one large

- Chopped tomatoes, two media sized
- Bean sprouts, one cup
- Fresh coriander leaves, half cup
- Fish sauce, one tbsp.
- Lime juice, two tbsp.
- Sliced red chili, one long
- Green beans, one cup

Instructions:

1. Whisk eggs, lime juice, fish sauce, quarter cup water and half of the chili in a large jug.

2. Heat two teaspoons of oil in a medium non-stick frying pan over medium-high heat. Cook mushrooms and capsicum, stir, for five minutes or until golden and tender.

3. Add tomato. Cook, stirring, for two minutes or until slightly softened. Meanwhile, place green beans in a heatproof bowl.

4. Cover with boiling water.

5. Wait for few minutes and then drain.

6. Rinse under cold water.

7. Combine mushroom mixture, beans and sprouts in a bowl.

8. Wipe the pan clean. Heat one teaspoon of remaining oil in pan over medium-high heat. Pour quarter of the egg mixture into pan.

9. Swirl to coat.

10. Cook for 30 seconds or until just set.

11. Slide omelet onto a plate.

12. Cover to keep warm.

13. Repeat with remaining oil and egg mixture to make 4 omelets.

14. Place quarter of the mushroom mixture over one half of each omelet.

15. Fold over to enclose filling.

16. Serve by sprinkling with coriander and remaining chili.

3.2 Yam Kai (Thai Eggs) with Leftover Grains Recipe

Cooking Time: 10 minutes

Serving Size: 2

Ingredients:

- Vegetable oil, one and a half tbsp.
- Cooked pork chops, one cup
- Eggs, four
- Sliced scallions, four
- Sliced shallots, two medium sized
- Cooked barley, one cup
- Fresh coriander leaves, half cup
- Fish sauce, one tbsp.
- Lime juice, two tbsp.
- Sliced red chili, one long

Instructions:

1. In a medium bowl, stir together the lime juice, fish sauce, one teaspoon of the chili, and the cooked grain of your choice.

2. Put the eggs and the remaining half teaspoon of chili paste in a small bowl and beat with a fork to combine.

3. In a large heavy sauté pan, heat half tablespoon of the oil over medium-high heat.

4. Add the shallots, the white sections of the scallions, and the pork, if using, and cook, stirring occasionally, until the shallots are very dark brown and shriveled for about four minutes.

5. Add the scallion greens and the remaining half tablespoon of oil and cook for one minute.

6. Pour in the egg mixture and cook without disturbing for thirty seconds, then turn and stir, breaking it up a little but keeping good-size pieces together, cooking until just set for about one minute.

7. Pour in the grain mixture and cook, turning with a spatula, until heated through for about one minute.

8. Your dish is ready to be served.

3.3 Thai Breakfast Rice Soup with Shrimp Recipe

Cooking Time: 10 minutes

Serving Size: 4

Ingredients:

- Soy sauce, one and a half tbsp.

- Pork stock, three cups

- Jasmine rice, four cups

- Garlic cloves, four

- White peppercorns, one tsp.

- Cilantro, one cup

- Shrimps, 150 grams
- Fish sauce, one tbsp.

Instructions:

1. Pound white peppercorns until fine, then add garlic and cilantro and pound until fine.

2. Add half of this paste to your small pieces of shrimps and mix well.

3. Sauté the small pieces of shrimp in a pan with a little bit of oil just until it is cooked through.

4. Deglaze the pan with some stock as needed and scrape any bits of herb stuck to the bottom.

5. Remove from pan and set aside.

6. If using whole garnish shrimp, sear the whole shrimp over medium high heat until browned and cooked through.

7. Bring the stock to a boil in a pot, add the other half of the herb paste and simmer for one minute.

8. Season with fish sauce and soy sauce, then taste and adjust seasoning.

9. When ready to serve, bring the broth to a boil then add the rice and the shrimp.

10. Bring the soup back to a simmer, and immediately turn off the heat.

11. Serve immediately, if you let this sit, the rice will continue to absorb liquid.

12. Ladle into a bowl, and top with all the condiments as desired.

3.4 Noodles Stuffed Thai Omelette Recipe

Cooking Time: 15 minutes

Serving Size: 4

Ingredients:

- Soy sauce, two tbsp.
- Eggs, eight
- Dried chilies, half tsp.
- Sesame oil, one tbsp.
- Cornstarch, one tsp.
- Button mushrooms, one cup
- Rice noodles, 150 grams
- Sesame seeds, one tbsp.
- White wine vinegar one tbsp.
- Green pepper, one
- Carrots, two
- Canola oil, six tbsp.
- White cabbage, one cup
- Fresh ginger, one tsp.
- Salt and pepper to taste

Instructions:

1. Mix the cornstarch with cold water in a bowl.
2. Add the eggs and whisk together until mixed.
3. Stir in the chilies and season with pepper.
4. Heat one teaspoon of the canola oil in a 20 cm nonstick frying pan over medium heat.

5. Pour in one-quarter of the egg mixture, tipping the pan to spread out the egg in a thin, even layer.

6. Cook for two minutes or until set and golden-brown.

7. Slide the omelet out of the pan onto a plate.

8. Make three more omelets in the same way, stacking them up interleaved with parchment paper.

9. Set aside and keep warm.

10. While making the omelets, soak the rice noodles in boiling water to cover for four minutes, or according to the package instructions, then drain.

11. Heat the remaining two teaspoons canola oil with the sesame oil in a wok or large frying pan.

12. Add the mushrooms, carrots, pepper and cabbage and stir-fry for few minutes or until just tender.

13. Add the soy sauce, vinegar, ginger and rice noodles.

14. Gently toss together until hot.

15. Divide the vegetable and noodle mixture among the Thai omelets and fold them over in half.

16. Sprinkle with the sesame seeds, if using, and serve immediately.

3.5 Thai Breakfast Rice Soup Recipe (Jok)

Cooking Time: 50 minutes

Serving Size: 2

Ingredients:

- Soy sauce, one and a half tbsp.
- Vegetable oil, half cup
- White vinegar, a quarter cup

- Long red chili, one
- Garlic cloves, ten
- Pork mince, 150 grams
- Long grain rice, one cup
- Scallions, to serve
- Garlic cloves, four
- Eggs, four
- White peppercorns, one tsp.
- Cilantro, one cup
- Fresh ginger, one tsp.
- Fish sauce, one tbsp.

Instructions:

1. Place eggs in a heat-proof bowl.
2. Pour over boiling water and allow to stay for ten minutes.
3. Remove eggs and set aside for later.
4. Rinse the rice briefly under running water.
5. Place the rice in a large saucepan with five cups of water.
6. Bring to boil over high heat, then reduce the heat to low and gently simmer for fifteen minutes.
7. Frequently use a wooden spoon to stir and break up the rice grains and to make sure that the rice is not sticking to the bottom of the pan.
8. The rice should be of a thick porridge consistency.
9. Meanwhile, make the pork balls.

10. Use a mortar and pestle to pound the garlic cloves to a paste.

11. Mix the garlic with the pork mince, pepper and fish sauce.

12. Heat four cups of water in a large pot over high heat.

13. When simmering, add teaspoonful of the pork mixture.

14. Simmer for three to four minutes or until the pork balls are cooked through. Remove from heat.

15. Season the stock with fish sauce and white pepper to taste.

16. For the garlic oil, heat the vegetable oil in a small saucepan over medium heat.

17. Add the garlic and gently fry for about two minutes or until just starting to turn golden.

18. Pour into a heat-proof jar or bowl and set aside until ready to serve.

19. For the chili vinegar, combine the chili and vinegar in a small bowl and set aside.

20. To serve, place the pork soup back onto high heat and bring to a simmer.

21. Add half of the rice porridge mixture and stir through.

22. Heat over medium-high heat until just simmering.

23. The soup should have a thick soupy consistency.

24. You can add more or less of the rice porridge mixture according to your taste. Crack one egg into each bowl and ladle the hot rice soup over the top.

25. Top the soup with coriander and spring onion.

26. Serve with fish sauce, ginger, garlic oil, chili vinegar, and pepper.

3.6 Spicy Thai Breakfast Noodles Recipe

Cooking Time: 25 minutes

Serving Size: 4

Ingredients:

- Chili garlic sauce, two tbsp.
- Fresh cilantro leaves, half cup
- Thai basil leaves, a quarter cup
- Beef broth, one can
- Minced lemon grass, one tsp.
- Egg, one large
- Rice stick noodles
- Thai chilies, two
- Jalapeno, one large
- Sliced green onions, half cup
- White peppercorns, one tsp.
- Cilantro, one cup
- Fresh ginger, one tsp.
- Fish sauce, one tbsp.
- Soy sauce, one tbsp.
- Chinese 5 spice, half tsp.

Instructions:

1. Slice vegetables.
2. Mix everything together in a large microwavable bowl.
3. Microwave for five minutes.
4. Make sure your broth is bubbling.

5. Add rice stick noodles to broth mixture.

6. Stir well.

7. The rice stick noodles are cooked in ten seconds in heated broth or water.

8. Quickly add an egg and mix well.

9. It will cook in the broth.

10. Garnish soup with additional fresh Cilantro and sesame seeds.

11. Serve with sides of Garlic Chili Sauce, Fish Sauce and Soy Sauce.

3.7 Pad Thai Omelette Recipe

Cooking Time: 10 minutes

Serving Size: 2

Ingredients:

- Tamarind paste, one and a half tbsp.
- Shrimps, two ounces
- Chili sauce, one tsp.
- Palm sugar, two tsp.
- Shitake mushrooms, two
- Bean sprouts, one cup
- Finely chopped shallot, one
- Eggs, four
- Oil, one tbsp.
- Sliced scallions, four
- Green onion, one

- Chopped roasted peanuts, one tbsp.
- Eggs, two
- Birds eye chili, one
- Fish sauce, two tbsp.
- Cilantro, to taste
- Butter, one tsp.

Instructions:

1. Heat the water, tamarind, fish sauce, sugar and chili until the sugar is dissolved and set aside.
2. Heat oil in a pan over medium-high heat.
3. Add the shrimp, shiitake, shallot and garlic and sauté for two minutes.
4. Add the sauce, bean sprouts, green onion and peanuts and cook for one minute.
5. Add the chili and cilantro and remove from heat and set aside.
6. Wipe out the pan and melt the butter over medium heat.
7. Mix the eggs and the fish sauce, pour them into the pan and cook until almost set, about two minutes.
8. Spoon the shrimp mixture onto half of the omelet and fold the other half over.
9. Your dish is ready to be served.

3.8 Boiled Eggs with Thai Dipping Sauce Recipe

Cooking Time: 10 minutes

Serving Size: 2- 4

Ingredients:

- Green onions, a quarter cup
- Eggs, five
- Red cayenne chili, two tbsp.
- Fish sauce, two tsp.
- Fresh lime juice, two tbsp.
- Erythritol sweetener, one tsp.

Instructions:

1. Place a medium sized pot quarter filled with water onto the stove.

2. Bring to boil.

3. Once water is being boiled, gently place the eggs into the hot water, and cook for five minutes.

4. While the eggs are being cooked, slice the green onions and chili, set aside.

5. Into a small bowl, mix together the lime juice, fish sauce and erythritol.

6. Remove the eggs from the hot water, run under cold water for one minute and peal shells.

7. Slice in half and place into a wide bowl.

8. Place the lime dipping sauce into the middle, and cover with green onions and chili.

9. Dip the eggs into the dipping sauce, and enjoy.

3.9 Thai Vegetable Omelette Recipe

Cooking Time: 10 minutes

Serving Size: 2

Ingredients:

- Water, two tbsp.
- Turmeric powder, one pinch
- Salt to taste
- Garlic cloves, four
- Eggs, two
- Mix veggies, one cup
- Olive oil

For Thai Dressing:

- Fish sauce, half tbsp.
- Brown sugar, half tbsp.
- Chopped small chili, one
- Water, one tbsp.
- Peanut oil, one tsp.
- Rice vinegar, half tbsp.
- Sweet chili sauce, half tbsp.

Instructions:

1. Heat up a cast iron skillet with some oil and quickly stir-fry garlic, bok choy, broccoli, asparagus, snow peas, mushrooms, and bean sprouts or any other vegetable of your choice.

2. Season with salt and pepper and cook until veggies are tender but still crisp. Set aside.

3. In a medium bowl, beat together the eggs, water, salt and turmeric.

4. Wipe the cast iron skillet clean with paper towel, and add a bit more oil.

5. Heat the skillet up again, and pour in the beaten eggs.

6. Cook over low heat until the eggs start to set.

7. Remove the skillet from the heat, while the hot skillet continues to cook the omelet further, top it with the cooked assorted vegetables, and then fold the omelet over them.

8. Drizzle with Thai dressing and serve with remaining dressing on the side.

3.10 Khai Yat Sai Recipe

Cooking Time: 10 minutes

Serving Size: 2

Ingredients:

- Scallions, four
- Mixed mushrooms, 250g
- Salt to taste
- Garlic cloves, one
- Eggs, four
- Cilantro, half cup
- Thai chili, half tsp.
- Thai basil, two springs
- Fish sauce, two tbsp.
- Oyster sauce, two tbsp.

- Black sesame seeds, two tbsp.
- Pepper to taste
- Vegetable oil, as required

Instructions:

1. Thinly slice scallions, separating the greens from the whites.

2. Mince the garlic. Roughly chop mushrooms and cilantro.

3. Mince the Thai chili.

4. In a frying pan, sauté chopped mushrooms with some vegetable oil until soft.

5. Add chopped garlic and scallion whites.

6. Add tomato paste over high heat and let fry shortly.

7. Season it with salt.

8. Add most of the chopped cilantro when it is almost done and mix together well.

9. Remove from heat and set aside.

10. In a bowl, whisk the eggs together with fish sauce, half of black sesame seeds, and chopped Thai chili.

11. Season with salt and pepper if necessary.

12. Pour half of the mixture into a big frying pan with hot oil to make a crepe.

13. Add half of the prepared mushroom mixture on one side of the crepe, and then fold it in half to form an omelet.

14. Repeat the process and make another omelet with the remaining egg and mushroom mixture.

15. Garnish with oyster sauce, scallion greens, Thai basil, remaining black sesame seeds and cilantro and serve.

3.11 Thai Scrambled Eggs Recipe

Cooking Time: 10 minutes

Serving Size: 4

Ingredients:

- Salt to taste
- Baby plum tomatoes, four
- Eggs, four
- Cilantro, half cup
- Spring onions, four
- Tortilla, as required
- Pepper to taste
- Butter, as required

Instructions:

1. Put the butter, spring onions and chili in a small pan.
2. Cook for a couple of minutes until softened.
3. Beat together the eggs and milk.
4. Add to the pan and cook them until scrambled.
5. Stir in the tomatoes and coriander leaves, if using.
6. Serve with griddled tortillas.

3.12 Kai Jeow Recipe

Cooking Time: 10 minutes

Serving Size: 1

Ingredients:

- Soy sauce, one tsp.
- Chopped scallions, one
- Eggs, two
- Cilantro, for garnish
- Salt to taste
- Sirarcha, as per taste
- Pepper to taste
- Olive oil, one tsp.

Instructions:

1. Heat the oil in a frying pan or wok until very hot.
2. Beat the eggs, chopped spring onion, soy sauce, salt and pepper.
3. Pour into the hot pan.
4. Cook for few minutes until lightly browned, flip and cook for further two minutes on the other side.
5. Serve immediately, drizzled with sriracha sauce to taste.

3.13 Thai Breakfast Baskets Recipe

Cooking Time: 20 minutes

Serving Size: 4

Ingredients:

- Minced green onion, one
- Minced jalapeno, a quarter cup

- Egg roll wrappers, eight
- Mango, one small
- Queso fresco, a quarter cup
- Avocado, one small
- Salsa Verde, a quarter cup
- Sesame oil, one tsp.
- Pumpkin seeds, to garnish
- Lime juice, one tsp.

Instructions:

1. Press wraps into nonstick muffin cups.

2. Bake at 375 degrees for seven minutes or till lightly browned and crisp.

3. Remove baskets from cups to wire rack to cool.

4. Combine remaining ingredients in medium sized bowl; fill each basket, dividing equally.

5. Garnish with pumpkin seeds and serve.

3.14 Thai Breakfast Bake Recipe

Cooking Time: 35 minutes

Serving Size: 4

Ingredients:

- Minced garlic, one tsp.
- Minced onion, one
- Diced tomatoes, one medium
- Grated potatoes, four cups
- Ground cumin, half tsp.

- Salt, half tsp.
- Ground coriander, half tsp.
- Red bell pepper, one small
- Coconut aminos, half tsp.
- Coconut milk, a quarter cup
- Ghee, one tsp.
- Eggs, four
- Lime juice, one tsp.

Instructions:

1. Preheat the oven to 350 degrees.
2. In a cast iron pan, melt the ghee over medium heat.
3. Add the onion, garlic, ginger, and red pepper and sauté until the onion starts to get translucent.
4. Add the coconut milk, coconut aminos, lime juice, spices, sand salt and mix.
5. Cook for another five minutes.
6. Add the tomato and sweet potato and mix well to combine.
7. Turn the stovetop off and transfer the pan to the oven and bake for twenty-five minutes.
8. Remove from the oven, and turn the oven to broil.
9. Make four little wells in the sweet potatoes and crack an egg in each.
10. Place the pan back in the oven on the top rack for five minutes depending on how you like your eggs to be cooked.
11. Your dish is ready to be served.

3.15 Thai Breakfast Bowl Recipe

Cooking Time: 1 minutes

Serving Size: 6

Ingredients:

- Chopped bell peppers, one
- Minced garlic, one
- Shredded carrots, five
- Toasted cashews, one cup
- Coconut milk, fourteen ounces
- Salt, half tsp.
- Shredded kale leave, two and a half cups
- Blackberries, one and a half cup
- Shredded Napa cabbage, two and a half cups
- Yellow curry powder, one tbsp.
- Ghee, one tsp.
- Garlic chili paste, one tsp.
- Lime juice, one tsp.

Instructions:

1. Place the dressing ingredients into a high-speed blender.
2. Blend on high speed for about 30 seconds, until smooth and creamy throughout.
3. Add salad ingredients to a large bowl and toss with as much dressing as you would like.
4. Add a little bit it at a time.

5. Serve right away.

3.16 Thai Breakfast Quesadilla Recipe

Cooking Time: 10 minutes

Serving Size: 2

Ingredients:

- Red bell peppers, a quarter cup
- Flour tortillas, two (12-inch size)
- Small green onion
- Thai peanut satay sauce, two tablespoons
- Grilled chicken (spicy seasoning optional), four ounces
- Reduced fat monetary jack cheese, half cup

Instructions:

1. Heat a skillet over medium-low heat.
2. Place two tortillas on a clean workspace.
3. Top one tortilla with Monterey Jack cheese, sliced chicken, peanut satay sauce, sliced red peppers, and green onions.
4. Place the second tortilla on top of the ingredients.
5. Spray top of the tortilla lightly with nonstick olive oil cooking spray.
6. Transfer quesadilla into preheated skillet.
7. Cook for five minutes, or until golden brown.
8. Spray top tortilla, and then flip in skillet.
9. Cook until golden brown.
10. Serve right away.

3.17 Thai French Toast Recipe

Cooking Time: 5 minutes

Serving Size: 6

Ingredients:

- Sweetened condensed milk, for garnish
- Eggs, two
- White bread, six slices
- Granulated sugar, two tablespoons
- Whole milk, half cup
- Vegetable oil, half cup
- Kosher salt, a pinch

Instructions:

1. In a medium bowl, whisk together the milk, eggs, sugar, and salt until combined.

2. Pour the mixture into a shallow dish, and then dip each slice of bread into the batter, stacking the slices and letting them sit in the dish while you heat the oil.

3. In a wok, heat the vegetable oil to 325 degrees and line a sheet pan with a wire rack.

4. Working with two slices at a time, shake off any excess batter, and fry, flipping once until golden brown, two minutes per side.

5. Transfer each slice to the prepared sheet pan to drain.

6. Divide the French toast between plates and top each piece with a heavy drizzle of sweetened condensed milk, and then serve.

3.18 Thai Breakfast Porridge Recipe

Cooking Time: 5 minutes

Serving Size: 4

Ingredients:

- Vegetable stock, six cups
- Sesame seeds, one tbsp.
- White rice, one cup
- Poached eggs, four
- Sautéed red cabbage, one cup
- Kimchi, half cup
- Chives, for garnish

Instructions:

1. Bring water to a boil and add the rice. Bring all ingredients to a simmer, and cover the pan.

2. Continue to simmer for thirty minutes until the rice porridge is very creamy.

3. While the rice is simmering, you can prepare the optional garnishes.

4. Remove from heat, add your desired garnishes, and serve warm.

Chapter 4: Thai Lunch and Dinner Recipes

Thai lunch and dinner recipes consist of amazing dishes that are healthy, nutritious and flavorful at the same time. Following are some amazing Thai lunch and dinner recipes that you can easily make at home:

4.1 Pad Thai Recipe

Cooking Time: 15 minutes

Serving Size: 4

Ingredients:

- Chopped green onions, three
- Eggs, two
- Fresh bean sprouts, half cup
- Garlic cloves, three
- Oil, three tbsp.

- Shrimp or chicken, eight ounces
- Limes, two
- Red bell pepper, one
- Flat rice noodles, eight ounces
- Dry roasted peanuts, two cups
- Soy sauce, one tbsp.
- Light brown sugar, five tbsp.
- Fish sauce, three tbsp.
- Creamy peanut butter, two tbsp.
- Rice vinegar, two tbsp.
- Sirarcha hot sauce, one tbsp.

Instructions:

1. Cook noodles according to package instructions, just until tender.
2. Rinse under cold water.
3. Mix the sauce ingredients together. Set aside.
4. Heat one and a half tablespoons of oil in a large saucepan or wok over medium-high heat.
5. Add the shrimp, chicken or tofu, garlic and bell pepper.
6. The shrimp will cook quickly, about two minutes on each side, or until pink.
7. If using chicken, cook until just cooked through, about five minutes, flipping only once.
8. Push everything to the side of the pan.
9. Add a little more oil and add the beaten eggs.
10. Scramble the eggs, breaking them into small pieces with a spatula as they cook.

11. Add noodles, sauce, bean sprouts and peanuts to the pan.

12. Toss everything to combine.

13. Top with green onions, extra peanuts, cilantro and lime wedges.

14. Your dish is ready to be served.

4.2 Easy Thai Noodles Recipe

Cooking Time: 25 minutes

Serving Size: 3

Ingredients:

- Coleslaw mix, one bag
- Green onions, a quarter cup
- Shredded carrots, half cup
- Honey roasted peanuts, half cup
- Oil, three tbsp.
- Rotisserie chicken, two cups
- Linguini noodles, five ounces
- Cilantro, a quarter cup
- Soy sauce, one tbsp.
- Honey, five tbsp.
- Sesame oil, three tbsp.
- Red chili flakes, two tbsp.
- Minced garlic, four

Instructions:

1. Cook linguini noodles according to the package instructions.

2. Drain when fully cooked.

3. While noodles are being cooked, whisk together in a small bowl, the soy sauce, honey, sesame oil, garlic and red pepper flakes.

4. Pour sauce onto drained noodles, and toss together.

5. Add shredded cabbage, shredded carrots and shredded cilantro to noodle mixture and mix.

6. Then gently stir in half of the chopped cilantro, green onions and peanuts, reserving the other half for garnish.

7. Serve warm or cold and garnish with remaining cilantro, green onions and chopped peanuts.

8. Your dish is ready to be served.

4.3 Thai Red Curry Recipe

Cooking Time: 20 minutes

Serving Size: 4

Ingredients:

- Coleslaw mix, one bag
- Green onions, a quarter cup
- Thai basil, half cup
- Kefir lime leaves, half cup
- Oil, one tbsp.
- Boneless chicken thigh, eight pieces

- Coriander, for garnish
- Soy sauce, one tbsp.
- Honey, five tbsp.
- Brown sugar, half tbsp.
- Red curry paste, five tbsp.
- Minced garlic and ginger, one tsp.
- Cooked jasmine rice

Instructions:

1. Heat one tablespoon of vegetable oil in a large saucepan over a medium heat and fry one tablespoon of ginger and one tablespoon of garlic paste for 2 minutes. Add the red curry paste, sizzle for a few seconds, and then pour in the coconut milk.

2. Bring to the boil, reduce to a simmer, stir a little and wait for the oil to rise to the surface.

3. Add the skinless, boneless chicken thighs, cut into chunks, and kaffir lime leaves, and simmer for twelve minutes or until the chicken is cooked through.

4. Add Soy sauce and a pinch of brown sugar, then taste if you like it a little saltier, add more Soy sauce; if you like it sweeter, add a little more sugar.

5. Bring to the boil, take off the heat and add Thai basil.

6. Spoon the curry into four bowls and top with the red chili, a thumb-sized piece of ginger and a few extra basil leaves.

7. Serve with jasmine rice.

4.4 Thai Green Chicken Curry Recipe

Cooking Time: 20 minutes

Serving Size: 2

Ingredients:

- Shredded carrots, two
- Green curry paste, a quarter cup
- Lime, half
- Cherry tomatoes, half cup
- Oil, one tbsp.
- Boneless chicken, eight pieces
- Coriander, for garnish
- Soy sauce, one tbsp.
- Coconut cream, five tbsp.
- Brown sugar, half tbsp.
- Uncooked jasmine rice, one pack

Instructions:

1. In a medium saucepan, bring the water to the boil.
2. Add the jasmine rice, stir, cover with a lid and reduce the heat to low.
3. Slice the carrot (unpeeled) into half-moons.
4. Roughly chop the coriander.
5. Slice the lime into wedges.
6. Cut the chicken breast into thin strips.
7. In a small bowl, combine the Thai green curry paste, coconut cream, the soy sauce, sugar, a good squeeze of lime juice and a drizzle of olive oil.

8. In a large frying pan, heat a drizzle of olive oil over a high heat.

9. When the oil is hot, add the chicken with a pinch of salt and pepper and cook, tossing, until browned and cooked through.

10. Transfer to a plate and repeat with the remaining chicken.

11. Add the Asian greens, carrot and Thai green curry paste and cook until fragrant.

12. Simmer the Vegetables.

13. Season to taste with salt and pepper.

14. Divide the jasmine rice between bowls and top with the Thai green chicken curry.

15. Sprinkle with some of the coriander and squeeze over lime juice to serve.

4.5 Thai Peanut Chicken and Noodles Recipe

Cooking Time: 30 minutes

Serving Size: 4

Ingredients:

- Rice vinegar, two tbsp.
- Sesame oil, one tbsp.
- Water, half cup
- Soy sauce, half cup
- Sirarcha hot sauce, one tbsp.
- Cucumber slices and roasted peanuts
- Coriander, for garnish

- Peanut oil, one tbsp.

- Chicken tenders, one pound

- Peanut butter, two tbsp.

- Minced garlic, half tbsp.

- Rice noodles, one pack

- Onion, one

Instructions:

1. For sauce, whisk together the wet ingredients.

2. Bring a large saucepan of water to a boil; remove from heat.

3. Add noodles; let stand until noodles are tender but firm, five minutes.

4. Drain; rinse with cold water and drain well.

5. In a large skillet, heat one tablespoon peanut oil over medium-high heat; sauté chicken until no longer pink, five minutes.

6. In the same pan, sauté onion in remaining oil over medium-high heat until tender.

7. Stir in sauce; cook and stir over medium heat until slightly thickened.

8. Add noodles and chicken; heat through, tossing to combine. If desired, top with cucumber and chopped peanuts.

9. Serve immediately.

4.6 Thai Salad with Walnut Butter Recipe

Cooking Time: 5 minutes

Serving Size: 6

Ingredients:

- Rice vinegar, two tbsp.
- Sesame oil, one tbsp.
- Soy sauce, half cup
- Sirarcha hot sauce, one tbsp.
- Red cabbage, three cups
- Cilantro, half cup
- Red pepper, one
- Walnut butter, two tbsp.
- Toasted walnuts, half cup
- Dry noodles, one pack
- Carrot, one

Instructions:

1. Cook noodles according to package, rinse and set aside.
2. Prepare sauce by whisking all of the ingredients together in a bowl.
3. Add noodles, sliced veggies, cilantro, and toasted walnuts to another large bowl.
4. Pour sauce on top of noodle and veggie bowl and toss till fully coated.
5. Add sesame seeds on top.
6. Serve cold.

4.7 Thai Chicken Fried Rice Recipe

Cooking Time: 30 minutes

Serving Size: 4

Ingredients:

- Fish sauce, two tbsp.
- Egg, one
- Soy sauce, half cup
- Cooked brown jasmine rice, three cups
- Tomatoes, two
- Cilantro, half cup
- Salt and pepper, to taste
- Vegetable oil, two tbsp.
- Thai chili peppers, three
- Toasted walnuts, half cup
- Chicken breast, eight ounces
- Onion, one
- Scallions, half cup
- Minced garlic, one tsp.

Instructions:

1. Heat a large nonstick wok over high heat.
2. Meanwhile, season chicken lightly with salt and pepper.
3. When the wok is very hot, add two teaspoons of the oil.
4. When the oil is hot, add the chicken and cook on high until it is browned all over and cooked through.
5. Remove chicken from wok and set aside, add the eggs, pinch of salt and cook a minute or two until done.

6. Add the remaining oil to the wok and add the onion, scallions and garlic.

7. Sauté for a minute, add the chili pepper if using, tomatoes and stir in all the rice.

8. Add the soy sauce and fish sauce stir to mix all the ingredients.

9. Keep stirring a few minutes, and then add egg and chicken back to the wok.

10. Adjust soy sauce if needed and stir well for another 30 seconds.

11. Your dish is ready to be served.

4.8 Thai Rice Noodles with Chicken and Asparagus Recipe

Cooking Time: 40 minutes

Serving Size: 4

Ingredients:

- Asparagus, half pound
- Brown sugar, one tbsp.
- Soy sauce, a quarter cup
- Fish sauce, one tbsp.
- Chili garlic sauce, one tbsp.
- Oil, two tbsp.
- Chicken breast, eight ounces
- Rice noodles, half pound
- Minced garlic, one tsp.

Instructions:

1. Pour noodles into bowl and cover with hot tap water.

2. Soak for twenty minutes.

3. Heat oil in large skillet over medium-high heat.

4. Add garlic and stir fry until golden.

5. Add fish sauce or salt and chicken.

6. Stir fry until done.

7. Add soy sauce, chili pepper sauce, and brown sugar.

8. Mix until sugar is dissolved.

9. Drain noodles and add to skillet along with asparagus.

10. Stir fry noodles until firm but tender.

11. Your dish is ready to be served.

4.9 Thai Green Curry Soup Recipe

Cooking Time: 20 minutes

Serving Size: 4

Ingredients:

- Sliced mushrooms, one cup
- Vegetable stock, four cups
- Broccoli florets, three cups
- Coconut milk, a quarter cup
- Brown sugar, one tbsp.
- Soy sauce, one tsp.
- Thai green curry paste, two tbsp.
- Sesame oil, two tbsp.
- Salt to taste

- Crushed peanuts, one tbsp.
- Spring onion greens, one tbsp.
- Rice noodles, half pound
- Fresh basil, half cup
- Lime, two
- Minced garlic, one tsp.

Instructions:
1. Heat oil in a saucepan.
2. Add the vegetables (broccoli, mushroom) and stir fry them over high heat for five minutes.
3. Transfer to a plate and set aside.
4. In the same saucepan, add the garlic, ginger, and green curry paste.
5. Sauté the curry paste for few minutes to combine it evenly with the oil.
6. Add the coconut milk, brown sugar, and soy sauce.
7. Stir until the curry paste is nicely dissolved.
8. Next, add the vegetable stock, salt, and stir to combine.
9. Taste and add more coconut milk for a milder taste or green chilies to make it spicy.
10. Add the vermicelli noodles.
11. Simmer the soup till noodles are cooked.
12. This takes five minutes over medium heat.
13. Once noodles are cooked, add stir fry vegetables and give the soup a good stir. At this stage, if the soup seems too thick add more vegetable stock to get the desired consistency, simmer, and turn off the heat.

14. Just before serving, garnish the soup with fresh herbs, crushed peanuts, and juice of lemon.

15. Serve the soup warm.

4.10 Thai Chicken Coconut Curry Recipe

Cooking Time: 25 minutes

Serving Size: 6

Ingredients:

- Yellow onion, one
- Ground coriander, one tbsp.
- Soy sauce, a quarter cup
- Fish sauce, one tbsp.
- Coconut milk, one cup
- Shredded carrots, one cup
- Garlic and ginger paste, one tbsp.
- Oil, two tbsp.
- Fresh spinach leaves, three cups
- Cilantro, a quarter cup
- Brown sugar, two tbsp.
- Salt and pepper to taste
- Thai red curry paste, three tbsp.
- Chicken breast, one pound
- Rice to serve
- Lime juice, two tbsp.

Instructions:

1. To a large skillet, add the oil, onion, and sauté over medium-high heat until the onions begin to soften for about five minutes; stir intermittently.

2. Add chicken and cook for about five minutes, or until chicken is done; flip and stir often to ensure even cooking.

3. Add the garlic, ginger, coriander, and cook for about one minute, or until fragrant; stir frequently.

4. Add the coconut milk, carrots, Thai curry paste, salt, pepper, and stir to combine.

5. Reduce the heat to medium, and allow mixture to gently boil for about five minutes, or until liquid volume has reduced as much as desired and thickens slightly.

6. Add the spinach, lime juice, and stir to combine.

7. Cook until spinach is wilted and tender.

8. Taste and optionally add brown sugar, additional curry paste, salt, and pepper to taste.

9. Evenly sprinkle with the cilantro and serve immediately.

4.11 Thai Crunch Salad with Peanut Butter Dressing Recipe

Cooking Time: 5 minutes

Serving Size: 4-6

Ingredients:

- Shredded green cabbage, two cups
- Shredded red cabbage, two cups

- Sliced red bell pepper, one cup
- Shredded carrots, one cup
- Sliced yellow bell pepper, one cup
- Shredded carrots, one cup
- Green onions, a quarter cup
- Toasted Almonds, half cup
- Honey, two tbsp.
- Cilantro, a quarter cup
- Brown sugar, two tbsp.
- Salt and pepper to taste
- Sesame oil, one tsp.
- Peanut butter, half cup
- Fish sauce, two tsp.
- Lime juice, two tbsp.

Instructions:

1. Combine all of the dressing ingredients in a high-powered blender and blend until smooth and creamy.
2. Add all of the salad ingredients to a large bowl.
3. Drizzle your desired amount of the peanut dressing over the salad.
4. Toss the salad until well combined and coated in the dressing.
5. Your dish is ready to be served.

4.12 Thai Basil Chicken Recipe

Cooking Time: 20 minutes

Serving Size: 6

Ingredients:

- Fresh Thai basil leaves, two cups
- Oyster sauce, two tsp.
- Honey, two tbsp.
- Boneless chicken, two pounds
- Brown sugar, two tbsp.
- Salt and pepper to taste
- Canola oil, one tsp.
- Lime juice, two tbsp.
- Lime wedges, 4
- Crushed red chili flakes, two tsp.
- Fish sauce, two tsp.
- Minced garlic, two tbsp.

Instructions:

1. In a large bowl, stir together sliced chicken, oyster sauce, soy sauce, fish sauce, lime juice and brown sugar until evenly coated.

2. Allow chicken to marinate while preparing the rest of the meal.

3. Heat canola oil in a large skillet or wok over medium-high heat.

4. Add garlic and red pepper flakes and sauté until fragrant for about thirty seconds.

5. Add chicken and sauce and increase heat to high.

6. Cook, stirring frequently, until chicken is cooked through and no longer pink for about five minutes.

7. Add basil leaves and continue to cook, stirring occasionally, until basil leaves have wilted for about four minutes.

8. Your dish is ready to be served.

4.13 Thai Fish Curry Recipe

Cooking Time: 30 minutes

Serving Size: 4

Ingredients:

- Coconut cream, two cups
- Coconut milk, one cup
- Barracuda fish, 800 g
- Salt, to taste
- Kaffir lime leaves, twenty
- Lemongrass, two stalks
- Turmeric, one tsp.
- Thai dry chilies, two
- Black pepper, one tsp.
- Shrimp paste, two tbsp.
- Lime wedges, 4
- Crushed red chili flakes, two tsp.
- Bean sprouts
- Lemon basil
- Chinese long beans

- Fresh rice noodles, two pounds
- Minced garlic, two tbsp.
- Deep fried chilies

Instructions:

1. Gut and clean the fish, then cut into medium sized pieces.

2. Bring a pot of water to boil, and then boil the fish for about ten minutes until fully cooked.

3. Remove the fish from the water, drain fully, and leave to cool.

4. Once the fish is cool, carefully take off the skin and debone all the meat from the fish, and flake the fish in your fingers so it is almost like deboned minced fish.

5. Discard the bones and skin.

6. Set aside the fish for later.

7. Cut off the ends of the lemongrass and tear off the outer few layers, then shave the lemongrass into small pieces.

8. Cut the turmeric into small pieces as well.

9. Then add the lemongrass, turmeric, garlic, and peppercorns, and pound for about thirty minutes until a relatively smooth paste.

10. Once the paste is pretty smooth, the final step is to add the shrimp paste, and pound and mix for another five minutes.

11. Set aside.

12. In a large pot or sauce pan, add all the coconut milk and curry paste, then turn on medium heat.

13. Stir gently, and only in one direction, making sure all the curry paste dissolves into the coconut milk.

14. Add the minced fish, season with salt, and tear the kaffir lime leaves in half and add them to the curry.

15. Keep stirring in one direction, and once it comes to a boil, turn down the heat.

16. Keep stirring gently for about five minutes once it comes to a boil.

17. Your dish is ready to be served.

4.14 Pork Pad Thai Recipe

Cooking Time: 15 minutes

Serving Size: 4

Ingredients:

- Chopped green onions, three
- Eggs, two
- Fresh bean sprouts, half cup
- Garlic cloves, three
- Oil, three tbsp.
- Limes, two
- Red bell pepper, one
- Flat rice noodles, eight ounces
- Dry roasted peanuts, two cups
- Soy sauce, one tbsp.
- Light brown sugar, five tbsp.
- Fish sauce, three tbsp.

- Creamy peanut butter, two tbsp.
- Rice vinegar, two tbsp.
- Sirarcha hot sauce, one tbsp.
- Pork strips, half pound

Instructions:

1. Place all sauce ingredients in a jar and shake until well combined.
2. Bring 4 quarts of water to a boil.
3. Remove from heat and drop noodles in.
4. Stir to separate and cover with a lid.
5. Let them soak for six minutes.
6. Heat two tablespoon oil in a large skillet over medium-high heat.
7. Add the garlic and pork strips and cook until evenly browned on all sides and fully cooked.
8. Add the sprouts, carrots, pepper, and noodles in with the pork and stir fry for one to two minutes.
9. Take the pan off the heat and mix in the sauce, green onions, and peanuts.
10. Top with cilantro and sesame seeds and serve.

4.15 Beef Pad Thai Recipe

Cooking Time: 15 minutes

Serving Size: 4

Ingredients:

- Chopped green onions, three
- Eggs, two

- Fresh bean sprouts, half cup
- Garlic cloves, three
- Oil, three tbsp.
- Limes, two
- Red bell pepper, one
- Flat rice noodles, eight ounces
- Dry roasted peanuts, two cups
- Soy sauce, one tbsp.
- Light brown sugar, five tbsp.
- Fish sauce, three tbsp.
- Creamy peanut butter, two tbsp.
- Rice vinegar, two tbsp.
- Sirarcha hot sauce, one tbsp.
- Beef strips, half pound

Instructions:

1. Place all sauce ingredients in a jar and shake until well combined.
2. Bring 4 quarts of water to a boil.
3. Remove from heat and drop noodles in.
4. Stir to separate and cover with a lid.
5. Let them soak for six minutes.
6. Heat two tablespoon oil in a large skillet over medium-high heat.
7. Add the garlic and beef strips and cook until evenly browned on all sides and fully cooked.

8. Add the sprouts, carrots, pepper, and noodles in with the beef and stir fry for one to two minutes.

9. Take the pan off the heat and mix in the sauce, green onions, and peanuts.

10. Top with cilantro and sesame seeds and serve.

4.16 Thai Chopped Salad with Sesame Garlic Dressing Recipe

Cooking Time: 5 minutes

Serving Size: 4-6

Ingredients:

- Shredded green cabbage, two cups
- Shredded red cabbage, two cups
- Sliced red bell pepper, one cup
- Shredded carrots, one cup
- Sliced yellow bell pepper, one cup
- Shredded carrots, one cup
- Green onions, a quarter cup
- Toasted Almonds, half cup
- Honey, two tbsp.
- Cilantro, a quarter cup
- Brown sugar, two tbsp.
- Salt and pepper to taste
- Sesame oil, one tsp.
- Sesame, half cup
- Fish sauce, two tsp.

- Garlic paste, two tbsp.

Instructions:

1. Combine all of the dressing ingredients in a high-powered blender and blend until smooth and creamy.

2. Add all of the salad ingredients to a large bowl.

3. Drizzle your desired amount of the sesame garlic dressing over the salad.

4. Toss the salad until well combined and coated in the dressing.

5. Your salad is ready to be served.

4.17 Quick Thai Salad Recipe

Cooking Time: 5 minutes

Serving Size: 4-6

Ingredients:

- Cucumber cubes, two cups
- Bean sprouts, two cups
- Spring onion, one cup
- Shredded carrots, one cup
- Fresh mint leaves
- Fresh basil leaves
- Brown sugar, two tbsp.
- Peanuts
- Lime juice, two tsp.
- Fish sauce, two tsp.

Instructions:

1. In a bowl, mix together the veg and herbs.

2. Make the dressing by mixing together the fish sauce, lime juice and sugar.

3. When ready to serve, pour the dressing over the salad, toss to coat and scatter over the peanuts.

4.18 Thai Chicken Salad Recipe

Cooking Time: 5 minutes

Serving Size: 8

Ingredients:

- Carrots, one cup
- Cucumber, one cup
- Bok choy, two cups
- Cucumber, one cup
- Fresh mint leaves
- Green cabbage, three cups
- Chicken breast, two pounds
- Peanuts, half cup
- Olive oil, two tsp.
- Fish sauce, two tsp.
- Chili garlic sauce, two tsp.
- Honey, one tbsp.
- Peanut butter, two tbsp.
- Soy sauce, two tsp.

Instructions:

1. Whisk all the ingredients for the dressing together in a bowl or give them a shake in a mason jar.

2. You can microwave the peanut butter for fifteen seconds to soften it for easier mixing, if needed.

3. Add all the salad ingredients to a large bowl along with the dressing.

4. Toss everything well and serve right away.

Chapter 5: Thai Dessert Recipes

This chapter contains amazing Thai dessert recipes that you can easily make in your kitchen without any stress.

5.1 Thai Coconut Pudding Cake Recipe

Cooking Time: 30 minutes

Serving Size: 8

Ingredients:

- Eggs, two
- Coconut milk, one cup
- Rice flour, half cup
- Vanilla extract, one tsp.
- Coconut extract, one tsp.
- Sugar, a quarter cup
- Dry shredded coconut

- Coconut cream

Instructions:

1. Place one cup coconut milk in a mixing bowl.
2. Crack in the eggs, and add a pinch of salt.
3. Beat well with a fork or whisk until smooth.
4. Sprinkle the rice flour over and beat until smooth.
5. Add the coconut extracts and sugar.
6. Taste-test the batter for sweetness, adding a little more sugar if desired. Grease 4 ramekins with a few drops of cooking oil.
7. Ladle the batter into these ramekins, filling to 3/4.
8. Place ramekins inside a long baking dish.
9. Pour some water into this dish so that it reaches the sides of the ramekins. Place carefully in the oven.
10. Bake at 375 degrees minutes, or until the cakes are set.
11. Add a dollop of the coconut cream and a sprinkling of toasted coconut, if desired.
12. Your cake is ready to be served.

5.2 Mango Sticky Rice Recipe

Cooking Time: 25 minutes

Serving Size: 4

Ingredients:

- Water, one and a half cup
- Ripe mangoes, two
- Thai sweet rice, one cup
- Coconut milk, one can

- Salt, a quarter tsp.
- Brown sugar, five tbsp.

Instructions:

1. Soak rice in one cup water for twenty minutes.
2. Do not drain the rice.
3. Add half cup more water, plus half can of the coconut milk, the salt, and one tablespoon of the brown sugar.
4. Stir well.
5. Add coconut milk, salt, and some of the brown sugar to the saucepan.
6. Bring to a gentle boil, and then partially cover with a lid.
7. Reduce heat to medium-low, or just until you get a gentle simmer.
8. Simmer thirty minutes, or until the coconut water is absorbed by the rice.
9. Turn off the heat but leave the pot on the burner with the lid on tight.
10. Allow it to stay for five minutes.
11. To make the sauce, warm the remaining coconut milk over medium-low heat.
12. Add three tablespoons of brown sugar, stirring to dissolve.
13. Taste-test sauce for sweetness, adding more sugar if desired.
14. Prepare the mangoes by cutting them open and slicing each into bite-sized pieces.
15. Scoop some warm rice into each serving bowl, and then drizzle lots of the sweet coconut sauce over the top.

16. It should look like an English pudding with custard sauce, with the rice whirling in sauce.

17. Arrange mango slices on the rice and finish with a drizzle of more sauce.

5.3 Kanom Tuy Recipe

Cooking Time: 25 minutes

Serving Size: 4

Ingredients:

- Coconut milk, one can
- Salt, a pinch
- Sugar, a quarter cup
- Rice flour, a quarter cup

Instructions:

1. Place coconut milk in non-stick skillet to medium heat.

2. Add rice flour to milk while milk is cold or warm but not hot and mix well.

3. Add sugar and pinch of salt.

4. Stir until mixture starts to get thick.

5. Add warm water and mix well then take it off the heat, pour into small Thai style ceramic dish.

6. Let it set in the fridge.

7. Your dish is ready to be served.

5.4 Khanom Krok Recipe

Cooking Time: 25 minutes

Serving Size: 4

Ingredients:

- Coconut milk, one can
- Salt, a pinch
- Sugar, a quarter cup
- Rice flour, a quarter cup
- Cooked jasmine rice, 50 g
- Water, one cup
- Shredded coconut, half cup

Instructions:

1. Whisk the rice flour, sugar and salt together until there are no more clumps of flour.
2. Add coconut milk and whisk until sugar is dissolved.
3. Heat pan at 325.
4. To test pan for readiness, sprinkle a bit of water onto the pan, and if it sizzles away immediately, it is hot enough.
5. Brush half of the holes with coconut oil.
6. Then add some of the filling by dunking the teaspoon right into the middle of the shell and wiggle it slightly.
7. After a minute or two of cooking, the cakes should be partially set, go ahead and add your toppings.
8. Your dish is ready to be served.

5.5 Bua Loy Recipe

Cooking Time: 25 minutes

Serving Size: 4

Ingredients:

- Coconut milk, one can
- Pandan water, half cup
- Sugar, a quarter cup
- Pandan leaf, one
- Salt, a quarter tsp.
- Rice flour, a quarter cup
- Sticky rice flour, 50 g
- Water, one cup
- Sweet potato, 50 g

Instructions:

1. To make the sweet potato dumplings, mash the steamed sweet potato and add sticky rice flour.
2. Knead until combined into sandy textured dough.
3. Add water, one teaspoon at a time, until the dough comes together with sheen.
4. This is typically five to six teaspoons.
5. Roll into small marble sized balls.
6. Prepare the pandan bua loy as above by mixing the pandan water with the sticky rice flour.
7. Add more flour if the dough is too thin, or more pandan water if too thick.
8. Roll the dough into marble sized balls.
9. Make the coconut milk soup by adding the coconut milk, both kinds of sugar, salt, and knotted pandan leaf to a small saucepan and simmer for a few minutes.
10. Do not boil.

11. Discard the pandan leaf.

12. Bring a pot of water to the boil and tip in all of the dumplings.

13. Boil for a minute, or until all of the balls are floating.

14. Strain with a spider or mesh strainer and divide up amongst some bowls.

15. Pour the warm sweetened coconut milk over and serve.

5.6 Tub Tim Grob Recipe (Red Rubies Dessert)

Cooking Time: 25 minutes

Serving Size: 4

Ingredients:

- Crushed ice
- Ripe jackfruit
- Coconut milk, one cup
- Pandan leaf, one
- Salt, a quarter tsp.
- Sugar, half cup
- Red food color, few drops
- Water, one cup
- Chestnuts, 50 g
- Tapioca starch, half cup

Instructions:

1. Cut water chestnuts into about one cm. cubes.

2. Add just enough water to cover chestnuts, and then add red food coloring until the water is bright red.

3. Boil pandan leaves in water for ten minutes.

4. Then add sugar and stir to dissolve.

5. Chill completely.

6. Boil coconut milk, salt, water and pandan leaves for five minutes.

7. Bring a big pot of water to a boil.

8. Meanwhile, drain the chestnuts and place in a mixing bowl.

9. Sprinkle about the tapioca starch and toss to coat.

10. Keep adding until all pieces are completely coated in starch and are not sticking together.

11. For a thin coating, you will need about a quarter cup total.

12. For thicker coating you may need up to half cup.

13. Once done, put them in a strainer and shake off excess starch.

14. Prepare an ice water bowl for chilling the rubies after cooking.

15. To cook the rubies, sprinkle half of the rubies into rapidly boiling water, then stir briefly.

16. Boil them for about few minutes.

17. Scoop out a small amount with a slotted skimmer then dunk them into the cold-water bowl, keeping them in the skimmer for a few seconds just until the coating settles into a clear gel.

18. To serve, put a scoop of the rubies into a serving bowl, add jackfruit or young coconut meat if using.

19. Spoon the syrup over, just until it almost covers the rubies.

20. Top with a couple of tablespoons of coconut milk.

21. Your dish is ready to be served.

5.7 Thai Custard Recipe

Cooking Time: 50 minutes

Serving Size: 4

Ingredients:

- Coconut cream, one cup
- Eggs, four
- Vanilla extract, one tsp.
- Palm sugar, half cup

Instructions:

1. Whisk the eggs.
2. Add the coconut cream and the palm sugar.
3. Add in the vanilla extract.
4. Put the custard in steam safe bowls.
5. Add the bowls into layered steamer.
6. Steam for fifty minutes or until the custard reaches 170 degrees
7. As the custard becomes firm, it will expand.
8. You can check to see if the custard is done by poking a toothpick into the custard.
9. Your dish is ready to be served.

5.8 Thai Banana in Coconut Milk Recipe

Cooking Time: 10 minutes

Serving Size: 2

Ingredients:

- Coconut milk, one cup
- Banana, four
- Salt, one tsp.
- Palm sugar, half cup

Instructions:

1. In a medium saucepan, bring the coconut milk to a gentle boil.
2. Add the sliced bananas and reduce the heat to a simmer.
3. Cook until the banana pieces are tender but not falling apart, stirring occasionally, about five minutes.
4. Add sugar and stir until it is fully dissolved.
5. Sprinkle with salt.
6. Serve warm.

5.9 Thai Pumpkin in Coconut Milk Recipe

Cooking Time: 10 minutes

Serving Size: 2

Ingredients:

- Coconut milk, one cup
- Pumpkin pieces, four
- Salt, one tsp.

- Palm sugar, half cup

Instructions:

1. In a medium saucepan, bring the coconut milk to a gentle boil.

2. Add the sliced pumpkins and reduce the heat to a simmer.

3. Cook until the pumpkin pieces are tender but not falling apart, stirring occasionally, about five minutes.

4. Add sugar and stir until it is fully dissolved.

5. Sprinkle with salt.

6. Serve warm.

5.10 Khanum Tako Recipe

Cooking Time: 10 minutes

Serving Size: 2

Ingredients:

- Screwpine leaves, thirty
- Water, three cups
- Chestnuts, twelve
- Palm sugar, half cup
- Coconut cream, two cups
- Corn flour, one tbsp.
- Rice flour, two tsp.
- Salt, half tsp.

Instructions:

1. Wash the screwpine leaves and wipe dry.
2. Prepare the screwpine leaf juice.
3. Cut the screwpine leaves into short lengths.
4. Place into a blender with the water and process until fine.
5. Strain the juice through a muslin cloth and discard the pulp.
6. Place the arrowroot flour, screwpine leaf juice, water and sugar in a saucepan. Mix well.
7. Cook, stirring over medium heat until the mixture is thick, shiny and translucent.
8. Add the chestnuts and mix well.
9. Remove from the heat.
10. Pour the arrowroot mixture evenly into the screwpine leaf cases until they are half-full.
11. Refrigerate for about thirty minutes until the arrowroot layer is set.
12. In the meantime, prepare the coconut cream topping.
13. Place the coconut cream into a clean saucepan and sift in the rice flour and corn flour.
14. Add the salt.
15. Mix well and cook over medium heat until the coconut cream is thickened.
16. Pour the coconut cream topping over the set arrowroot layer.
17. Set aside to cool and set.
18. Serve chilled or at room temperature.

5.11 Red Sticky Rice Recipe

Cooking Time: 10 minutes

Serving Size: 2

Ingredients:

- Palm sugar, one cup
- Glutinous rice, one cup
- Coconut cream, two cups
- Sesame seeds

Instructions:

1. Wash and soak the glutinous rice for at least three hours.
2. Drain and steam the rice for ten mins.
3. In a brass wok or a heavy-base pan add palm sugar and stir until the sugar is dissolved then add coconut cream followed by salt.
4. When the sugar and coconut cream has merged and thickened add cooked rice and stir for around ten minutes.
5. Wait for the rice to cool down and transfer it to a tray. Add sesame seeds on top.
6. Now your caramel rice is ready to eat.

5.12 Thai Pumpkin Pudding Recipe

Cooking Time: 40 minutes

Serving Size: 4-6

Ingredients:

- Tapioca flour, one cup

- Rice flour, half cup
- Pumpkin, three cups
- Coconut cream, half cup
- Arrowroot starch, half tbsp.
- Salt, half tsp.
- Sugar, half cup

Instructions:

1. Mix tapioca flour, rice flour and arrowroot starch together.
2. Gradually add coconut cream, stir constantly until all the coconut cream is used up.
3. It will take about fifteen minutes.
4. Add sugar, pumpkin, salt and coconut milk; continue stirring until sugar and salt are all dissolved.
5. Pour the mixture into a baking pan, spread out evenly, steam over boiling water for twenty minutes or until done.
6. Remove from the heat and allow to cool.
7. Your dish is ready to be served.

5.13 Thai Black Rice Pudding Recipe

Cooking Time: 120 minutes

Serving Size: 4-6

Ingredients:

- Cold water, one cup
- Black rice, one cup
- Salt, half tsp.

- Sugar, half cup
- Coconut milk, one cup

Instructions:

1. Place rice in a bowl and rinse with water by stirring in a counter clockwise motion.

2. Do this repeatedly until the water is clear and clean, indicating the rice is clean.

3. Pick out any odd grains.

4. In a medium saucepan, stir rice, salt, sugar and water and bring to a boil.

5. Stir well and reduce heat to low.

6. Cover and simmer gently for two hours until all of the water has been absorbed and the rice is tender.

7. Stir in the coconut milk and serve immediately as a hot dish.

5.14 Thai Coconut Sticky Rice Recipe

Cooking Time: 25 minutes

Serving Size: 4

Ingredients:

- Water, one and a half cup
- Thai sweet rice, one cup
- Coconut milk, one can
- Salt, a quarter tsp.
- Brown sugar, five tbsp.

Instructions:

1. Soak rice in one cup water for twenty minutes.

2. Do not drain the rice.

3. Add half cup more water, plus half can of the coconut milk, the salt, and one tablespoon of the brown sugar.

4. Stir well.

5. Coconut milk, salt, and some of the brown sugar are added to the saucepan.

6. Bring to a gentle boil, and then partially cover with a lid.

7. Reduce heat to medium-low, or just until you get a gentle simmer.

8. Simmer for thirty minutes, or until the coconut water has been absorbed by the rice.

9. Turn off the heat but leave the pot on the burner with the lid on tight.

10. Allow it to stay for five minutes.

11. Let simmered sticky rice remain in the saucepan.

12. To make the sauce, warm the remaining coconut milk over medium-low heat.

13. Add three tablespoons of brown sugar, stirring to dissolve.

14. Taste-test sauce for sweetness, adding more sugar if desired.

15. Your dish is ready to be served.

5.15 Thai Tea Pudding Recipe

Cooking Time: 25 minutes

Serving Size: 4

Ingredients:

- Condensed milk, one and a half cup
- Thai tea leaves, three tbsp.
- Coconut milk, one can
- Vanilla extract, a quarter tsp.
- Cornstarch, five tbsp.

Instructions:

1. Heat one cup milk to a simmer.
2. Add the Thai tea and let steep for three minutes, no longer or it could become bitter.
3. Drain through a fine sieve.
4. In a sauce pan, whisk together the cornstarch, tea infused milk and remaining milk, condensed milk and vanilla.
5. Place over medium-low heat and bring to a low boil, stirring constantly.
6. Set heat for a constant low boil.
7. Stir constantly for one and a half minutes, scraping the sides and bottom of the pan.
8. Remove from the heat and pour into four pudding cups.
9. Let cool, then refrigerate.
10. Serve cold.

5.16 Thai Sweet Corn Pudding Recipe

Cooking Time: 50 minutes

Serving Size: 4

Ingredients:

- Water, two cups
- Corn ears, three
- Coconut milk, one can
- Vanilla extract, a quarter tsp.
- Sugar, five tbsp.
- Salt, half tsp.
- Tapioca peals, half cup
- Tapioca starch, half tsp.

Instructions:

1. Combine corn cobs and two cups of water in a pot.
2. Bring to a boil.
3. Cover and reduce heat to low and simmer for thirty minutes.
4. Meanwhile, cover tapioca pearls with a half inch of cold water and let stand.
5. Remove corn cobs from hot water and discard.
6. Add corn kernels, coconut milk, sugar, and salt to the pot.
7. Stir to combine. Return to a boil and then simmer for ten minutes.
8. Drain tapioca pearls and add them to pot.
9. Simmer for one minute.

10. Dissolve cornstarch in one tablespoon of water.

11. Remove from heat to cool down.

12. Serve at room temperature or chilled.

5.17 Thai Peanut Ice-cream Recipe

Cooking Time: 45 minutes

Serving Size: 8

Ingredients:

- Cream cheese, two cups
- Corn syrup, two tbsp.
- Coconut milk, four tbsp.
- Vanilla extract, a quarter tsp.
- Sugar, five tbsp.
- Salt, half tsp.
- Peanut butter, half cup
- Salt, half tsp.

Instructions:

1. Mix the coconut milk with the cornstarch in a small bowl to make smooth slurry. Using a hand mixer or a stand mixer with the whisk attachment, mix the cream cheese, peanut butter, and salt in a medium metal bowl until smooth.

2. Combine the remaining coconut milk, sugar, corn syrup, and honey in a 4-quart saucepan, bring to a rolling boil over medium-high heat, and boil for four minutes.

3. Remove from the heat and gradually whisk in the coconut milk cornstarch slurry. Bring this mixture back

to a boil over medium-high heat and cook, stirring once in a while with a spatula, until slightly thickened, about one minute.

4. Remove the pot from the heat.

5. Whisking, gradually pour the hot milk mixture into the peanut butter mixture.

6. Refrigerate for an hour and serve cold.

5.18 Thai Black Beans in Coconut Milk Recipe

Cooking Time: 10 minutes

Serving Size: 2

Ingredients:

- Coconut milk, one cup
- Black beans, one cup
- Salt, one tsp.
- Palm sugar, half cup

Instructions:

1. In a medium saucepan, bring the coconut milk to a gentle boil.

2. Add the black beans and reduce the heat to a simmer.

3. Cook until the black beans are tender but not falling apart, stirring occasionally, about five minutes.

4. Add sugar and stir until it is fully dissolved.

5. Sprinkle with salt.

6. Serve warm.

Chapter 6: Thai Famous and Alternative Recipes

This Chapter contains those famous and alternative Thai recipes that are known worldwide and eaten only by real Thai People and you have been longing to make them in your kitchen.

6.1 Thai Chicken Risotto Recipe

Cooking Time: 40 minutes

Serving Size: 6

Ingredients:

- Lime wedges
- Shallots, for garnish
- Green beans, 200g
- Fish sauce, two tbsp.
- Coconut cream, two tbsp.
- Minced garlic, one tsp.

- Arborio rice, one and a half cup
- Thai red curry paste, half cup
- Skinless chicken thigh filets, 500g
- Peanut oil, one tbsp.
- Red chili, one
- Onion, one
- Kaffir lime leaves, four

Instructions:

1. Preheat the oven to 180 degrees.
2. Heat the oil in a flameproof casserole over medium-high heat.
3. In batches, add the chicken and cook, turning, for few minutes until browned. Remove the chicken from the casserole and set aside.
4. Reduce heat to medium and add the onion, chili, garlic and half the kaffir lime leaves.
5. Cook, stirring constantly, for few minutes until the onion is soft, then add the rice and curry paste and cook, stirring to coat the grains, for a further one minute.
6. Return the chicken to the casserole with the stock and half cup water.
7. Bring to a simmer, then cover with a lid and cook in the oven for twenty-five minutes or until most of the liquid has been absorbed.
8. Remove from the oven and stir in the coconut cream, fish sauce and beans, then cover and let it stay for ten minutes.

9. Top risotto with coriander, fried Asian shallots and remaining kaffir lime leaves and serve with lime halves.

6.2 Thai Chicken Meatballs Recipe

Cooking Time: 20 minutes

Serving Size: 4

Ingredients:

- Lime wedges
- Fish sauce, two tbsp.
- Fresh mint leaves, two tbsp.
- Minced garlic and ginger, one tsp.
- Thai red curry paste, half cup
- Chicken mince, 500g
- Brown sugar, one tbsp.
- Red chili, one
- Kaffir lime leaves, four

Instructions:

1. Combine mince, garlic, ginger, kaffir lime leaves, mint and coriander in a bowl.
2. Using clean hands, roll the leveled tablespoons of mixture into balls.
3. Place on a large plate.
4. Refrigerate for thirty minutes.
5. Meanwhile, place fish sauce, lime juice, sugar and chili in a small bowl.
6. Stir until sugar dissolves.

7. Heat oil in a large, non-stick frying pan over medium heat.

8. Cook meatballs, in two batches, turning, for ten minutes or until light golden and cooked through.

9. Serve with dipping sauce and lime wedges, sprinkled with extra mint springs.

6.3 Hot and Sour Noodle Soup with Prawns Recipe

Cooking Time: 15 minutes

Serving Size: 4

Ingredients:

- Lime wedges
- Fish sauce, two tbsp.
- Tamarind paste, two tbsp.
- Minced garlic and ginger, one tsp.
- Glass noodles, 500g
- Water, four cups
- Tomatoes, two
- Red chili, one
- Prawns, 500g
- Snake beans, one cup
- Kaffir lime leaves, four

Instructions:

1. Place the stock, kaffir lime leaves, chili, ginger, fish sauce, tamarind paste, and water in a large heavy-based saucepan, and bring to the boil over high heat.

2. Reduce heat to medium-low and simmer for five minutes.

3. Meanwhile, place the glass noodles or vermicelli in a large heatproof bowl and pour over enough boiling water to cover.

4. Set aside for three minutes to soften, then rinse and drain well and divide among serving bowls.

5. Add the green or snake beans to the soup and simmer for a further two minutes.

6. Add the tomatoes and prawns, and then remove from the heat.

7. Wait for one minute until prawns are just cooked, then ladle soup over the noodles and garnish with coriander.

8. Serve immediately, with lime cheeks if desired.

6.4 Thai Coconut Soup with Prawns and Mushrooms Recipe

Cooking Time: 15 minutes

Serving Size: 2

Ingredients:

- Lime wedges
- Lemon grass, two sticks
- Fish sauce, two tbsp.
- Mushrooms, one cup
- Coconut milk, one cup
- Prawns, 500g
- Galangal, one can

- Chicken stock, two cups
- Minced garlic, one tsp.
- Palm sugar, two tbsp.
- Shallot, one
- Kaffir lime leaves, four

Instructions:

1. Bruise the chilies and repeatedly hit the lemongrass with the back of a knife, trimming the top and bottom ends and removing the outer layer if dirty or tough.

2. Add them and the coconut milk to a pan on low-medium heat and then tear the kaffir lime leaves and drop them in as well.

3. Reduce the coconut milk all the way down until it splits.

4. Remove the aromatics just before that occurs.

5. As the coconut milk reduces, peel and slice the shallot and three cloves of garlic. Slice the mushroom, as well, into suitable size of pieces.

6. Fry off the shallot, garlic and mushrooms in the coconut oil that has formed in the pan, increasing the heat to medium high.

7. Cook until the onions are soft and translucent.

8. Add the prawns and stir, flash cooking to get some color on the outside.

9. Add the stock and stir everything together, cooking for further five minutes.

10. Stir in some palm sugar and season with fish sauce and lime juice, to taste.

11. Garnish with basil and a wedge of lime.

6.5 Thai Som Tum without Papaya Recipe

Cooking Time: 15 minutes

Serving Size: 2

Ingredients:

- Lime wedges
- Unsalted cashews, two cups
- Fish sauce, two tbsp.
- Thai chili paste, one tbsp.
- Shredded carrot, one cup
- White cabbage, one cup
- Green snake beans, two cups
- Minced garlic, one tsp.
- Palm sugar, two tbsp.
- Bird's eye chili, one

Instructions:

1. In a small pan, dry roast cashews over medium high heat, tossing frequently. Roast until nuts are nearly blackened in small spots for about four minutes.

2. Combine the lime juice, chili paste, fish sauce and sugar in a small bowl.

3. Whisk to combine evenly.

4. Using a mortar and pestle, gently pound the garlic and bird's eye chili until both are crushed and broken into small pieces.

5. Add carrot and beans to the mortar and pound until carrots are moist and beans are crushed.

6. Pour contents of mortar into a small bowl.

7. Add cabbage and cashews.

8. Add liquid into the bowl bits at a time until vegetables are heavily dressed, stirring to combine.

9. Serve immediately or refrigerate and serve within a couple of hours, garnished with lime wedges.

6.6 Thai Green Curry Coconut Sauce Recipe

Cooking Time: 15 minutes

Serving Size: 2

Ingredients:

- Thai green curry paste, two tbsp.
- Unsweetened coconut milk, one cup
- Fish sauce, two tbsp.
- Lime juice, one tbsp.
- Fresh basil, one cup
- Chicken stock, one cup
- Minced ginger, one tsp.
- Brown sugar, two tbsp.
- Cilantro, a quarter cup

Instructions:

1. In a medium saucepan, whisk a quarter cup of the coconut milk with the curry paste.

2. Stir in the remaining coconut milk, the stock, lemon zest, ginger, lime zest, two tablespoons of the fish sauce and the brown sugar and bring to a simmer.

3. Cook the sauce over moderately high heat until reduced by one-quarter for about fifteen minutes.

4. Using a slotted spoon, remove the lemon zest, ginger and lime zest and discard. Stir in the lime juice, cilantro, basil and the remaining one tablespoon of fish sauce; transfer to a bowl.

5. Your curry paste is ready to serve.

6.7 Thai Pandan Chicken Recipe

Cooking Time: 20 minutes

Serving Size: 4

Ingredients:

- Pandan leaves, sixteen
- Skinless chicken thighs, 350 grams
- Fish sauce, two tbsp.
- Coriander roots, four
- Soy sauce, two tbsp.
- White peppercorns, half tsp.
- Oyster sauce, two tbsp.
- Minced garlic, one tsp.
- Coconut milk, two tbsp.
- Tamarind juice, one tbsp.
- Sesame seeds, one tbsp.
- Sirarcha hot sauce, one tbsp.

Instructions:

1. With a pestle and mortar, pound and grind coriander roots, garlic, white peppercorns, one teaspoon of light soy sauce, two tablespoons of oyster sauce and two tablespoon of coconut cream until well combined.

2. In a bowl, mix chicken pieces with marinade until evenly coated.

3. Let it marinate for thirty minutes.

4. In a small pot, on high heat, mix palm sugar, one tablespoon of sweet soy sauce, one tablespoon of light soy sauce, one tablespoon of sriracha hot sauce and one tablespoon of tamarind juice until sugar dissolves and sauce thickens.

5. Set aside to cool and transfer to the sauce dish.

6. Twist the middle part of the pandan leaf to prepare a pocket where you can put a piece of marinated chicken.

7. Wrap the pandan leaf around the chicken by looping the ends of the leaves into the pocket. Cut off any excess leaf.

8. In a pan or pot on medium-high heat, heat up enough oil for deep frying. When the oil is hot enough, about 180 degrees Celsius, deep-fry wrapped chicken for four minutes until the chicken is golden brown.

9. Remove deep-fried pandan-wrapped chicken from hot oil and place on a plate lined with a paper towel to drain excess oil.

10. Place Thai pandan chicken on a serving plate.

11. Sprinkle sesame seeds on the dipping sauce.

12. Serve hot with dipping sauce on the side.

6.8 Thai Beef Salad Recipe

Cooking Time: 5 minutes

Serving Size: 2

Ingredients:

- Tomatoes, two
- Cucumber, two
- Onion, one
- Mint leaves, a handful
- Basil leaves, a handful
- Lime leaves, a handful
- Oyster sauce, two tbsp.
- Barbequed beef strips, half pound
- Thai dressing, as required

Instructions:

1. Place the tomato, cucumber, onion, chili, mint, coriander, basil, peanuts and lime leaves in a large bowl.
2. Place beef strips in the salad.
3. Drizzle the dressing and gently toss to combine.
4. Divide salad among bowls and serve immediately.

6.9 Thai Mango Salad Recipe

Cooking Time: 5 minutes

Serving Size: 2

Ingredients:

- Tomatoes, two
- Cucumber, two
- Onion, one
- Mint leaves, a handful
- Basil leaves, a handful
- Lime leaves, a handful
- Oyster sauce, two tbsp.
- Mango chunks, one cup
- Thai dressing, as required

Instructions:

1. Place the tomato, cucumber, onion, chili, mint, coriander, basil, peanuts and lime leaves in a large bowl.
2. Put mango chunks in the salad.
3. Drizzle the dressing and gently toss to combine.
4. Divide salad among bowls and serve immediately.

6.10 Thai Spicy Lemongrass Soup Recipe

Cooking Time: 25 minutes

Serving Size: 2

Ingredients:

- Tomatoes, two
- Mushrooms, half cup
- Chicken strips, one cup
- Galangal, one cup

- Lemon grass, three

- Cilantro, half cup

- Makrut lime leaves, a handful

- Oyster sauce, two tbsp.

- Fish sauce, two tbsp.

- Thai dressing, as required

Instructions:

1. Whisk together the fish sauce, lime or lemon juice and chili paste in a small bowl.

2. Combine the lemongrass, galangal, makrut lime leaves and water or broth in a medium saucepan over high heat.

3. Bring to a boil; cook for few minutes, then use a slotted spoon to discard the solids.

4. Add the chicken to the pan, making sure the pieces do not stick together.

5. Once the liquid returns to a boil, add the mushrooms and tomatoes.

6. Cook for few minutes, until the chicken is cooked through and the tomatoes get softened, reducing the heat as needed to keep the soup from boiling over.

7. Remove from the heat; stir in the fish sauce mixture, scallion and cilantro. Serve hot.

6.11 Thai Grilled Salmon Recipe

Cooking Time: 25 minutes

Serving Size: 2

Ingredients:

- Salmon fillet, two pounds
- Lemon, two, cut in halves
- Butter, half cup
- Thai seasoning, two tbsp.
- Steamed rice, two cups
- Parsley, half cup
- Minced garlic, one tsp.
- Salt and pepper to taste

Instructions:

1. Season the salmon with salt, pepper, and Thai seasoning, rubbing them well on both sides.

2. Allow the salmon to briefly marinade on a slotted tray, at least for fifteen minutes.

3. Place the salmon on the grill skin side down and brush with oil on both sides. You may also use cooking spray.

4. Cook the salmon, flipping it regularly until it is cooked through.

5. Bring your butter out from the chiller and slice a half cm. thick ring.

6. Return any excess back to the chiller, and discard any paper wrapping of the cut portion.

7. Once the salmon is cooked, serve it with rice, lemon wedges, garlic butter on top, and your choice of vegetables.

6.12 Thai Cucumber Salad Recipe

Cooking Time: 5 minutes

Serving Size: 4-6

Ingredients:

- Cucumber, eight
- Toasted Almonds, half cup
- Honey, two tbsp.
- Cilantro, a quarter cup
- Brown sugar, two tbsp.
- Salt and pepper to taste
- Sesame oil, one tsp.
- Peanut butter, half cup
- Fish sauce, two tsp.
- Lime juice, two tbsp.

Instructions:

1. Combine all of the dressing ingredients in a high-powered blender and blend until smooth and creamy.
2. Add all of the salad ingredients to a large bowl.
3. Drizzle your desired amount of the dressing over the salad.
4. Toss the salad until well combined and coated in the dressing.
5. Your dish is ready to be served.

6.13 Thai Turkey Meatballs Recipe

Cooking Time: 20 minutes

Serving Size: 4-6

Ingredients:

- Lime zest, two
- Turkey leg piece, 500g
- Spring onions, three
- Cilantro, a quarter cup
- Chopped coriander, a handful
- Lime wedges
- Micro leaves
- Garlic cloves, two

Instructions:

1. Simply mix all the ingredients together.
2. Form into eight patties and leave in the fridge for twenty mins to rest and for the flavors to blend.
3. For cooking, either use the barbecue or gently fry in a little oil.
4. Scatter over the herbs and serve with lime wedges.

6.14 Thai Red Curry Paste Recipe

Cooking Time: 10 minutes

Serving Size: 6

Ingredients:

- Cumin seeds, two teaspoons

- Medium red chilies, four
- Garlic cloves, four
- Coriander seeds, two teaspoons
- Chopped coriander, a handful
- Hot paprika, two tsp.
- Grated lemon zest, two
- Lemon grass, four stems

Instructions:

1. Begin by splitting the chilies in half and removing and discarding the seeds.

2. Now take a small frying pan and pre-heat it over a medium heat, then add the coriander and cumin seeds and toss them around in the dry pan to roast them and draw out their flavors.

3. After about five minutes tip them into a mortar and crush them finely to a powder.

4. Now simply place the chilies, spices and all the other ingredients in a food processor and whiz them to a coarse paste.

5. Then freeze in the portions of two tablespoons.

6.15 Thai Seafood Soup Recipe

Cooking Time: 120 minutes

Serving Size: 2

Ingredients:

- Fish sauce, two tbsp.
- Mix seafood, three cups

- Garlic cloves, four
- Coriander seeds, two teaspoons
- Chopped coriander, a handful
- Hot paprika, two tsp.
- Grated lemon zest, two
- Kaffir lime leaves, four

Instructions:

1. Mix all the ingredients together and cover them to simmer in 2 liters of water for two hours.
2. Your soup is ready to be served.

6.16 Thai Peanut Sauce Recipe

Cooking Time: 10 minutes

Serving Size: 6

Ingredients:

- Peanut butter, half cup
- Garlic and ginger paste, half tsp.
- Water, as required
- Unseasoned rice vinegar, one tbsp.
- Maple syrup, one tbsp

Instructions:

1. Mix all the ingredients together.
2. Pour the mixture in a jar and store.
3. Use your sauce on anything you prefer.

6.17 Thai Chicken Soup Recipe

Cooking Time: 50 minutes

Serving Size: 2

Ingredients:

- Soy sauce, one and a half tbsp.
- Vegetable oil, half cup
- White vinegar, a quarter cup
- Long red chili, one
- Garlic cloves, ten
- Chicken mince, 150 grams
- Scallions, to serve
- Garlic cloves, four
- White peppercorns, one tsp.
- Cilantro, one cup
- Fresh ginger, one tsp.
- Fish sauce, one tbsp.

Instructions:

1. Mix all the ingredients together and cover them to simmer in 1.5 liters of water for fifty minutes.
2. Your soup is ready to be served.

6.18 Thai Turkey Soup Recipe

Cooking Time: 50 minutes

Serving Size: 2

Ingredients:

- Soy sauce, one and a half tbsp.
- Vegetable oil, half cup
- White vinegar, a quarter cup
- Long red chili, one
- Garlic cloves, ten
- Turkey mince, 150 grams
- Scallions, to serve
- Garlic cloves, four
- White peppercorns, one tsp.
- Cilantro, one cup
- Fresh ginger, one tsp.
- Fish sauce, one tbsp.

Instructions:

1. Mix all the ingredients together and cover it to simmer in 1.5 liters of water for fifty minutes.
2. Your soup is ready to be served.

Chapter 7: Thai Vegetarian and Slow Cooker Recipes

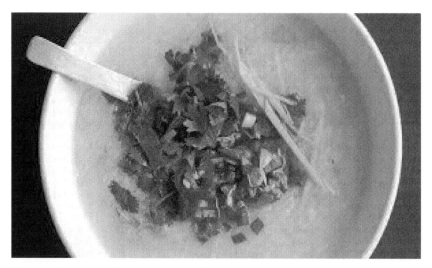

This chapter focuses on Thai vegetarian and slow cooker recipes that you will find very easy to make on your own.

7.1 Rainbow Vegetarian Pad Thai with Peanuts and Basil Recipe

Cooking Time: 5 minutes

Serving Size: 4

Ingredients:

- Fresh Thai herbs, half cup
- Zucchini, one
- Red bell pepper, one
- Eggs, one
- Carrots, two
- Brown rice noodles, four ounces

- Peanuts, half cup
- Vegetable oil, two tbsp.
- Basil sauce, as required

Instructions:

1. Place the uncooked noodles in a bowl of cold water to soak.
2. Cut the zucchini, red pepper, and onion into noodle-like shapes.
3. Shake up the sauce ingredients in a jar.
4. Heat a tablespoon of oil over medium high heat.
5. Add the veggies and stir fry with tongs.
6. Add another tablespoon of oil to the pan.
7. Add the noodles to the hot pan and stir fry for a minute, using tongs to toss. Add the basil sauce and stir fry for another minute or two, until the sauce starts to thicken and stick to the noodles.
8. Add eggs into the mixture and cook.
9. Add in the vegetables, toss together, and remove from heat.
10. Stir in the peanuts and herbs and serve immediately.

7.2 Thai Vegetarian Green Curry Recipe

Cooking Time: 40 minutes

Serving Size: 4

Ingredients:

- Salt, a pinch
- Red bell pepper, one

- Coconut milk, one cup
- Red bell pepper, one
- Thai green curry paste, four tbsp.
- Butternut squash, one
- Vegetable oil, two tbsp.
- Chili, one tsp.
- Water, 200ml
- Shallots, half cup
- Brown rice, four

Instructions:

1. Add the shallots with a pinch of salt and fry for ten mins over a medium heat until softened and beginning to caramelize.

2. Add the curry paste and chili to the dish and fry for two mins.

3. Tip in the squash and pepper, and then stir through the coconut milk along with 200ml water.

4. Season and stir through half of the coriander. Spoon the curry into deep bowls, scatter with the remaining coriander and serve with rice and lime wedges for squeezing over.

7.3 Vegetarian Coconut Curry Recipe

Cooking Time: 40 minutes

Serving Size: 4

Ingredients:

- Corn, half cup

- Salt, a pinch
- Coconut milk, one cup
- Vegetable oil, two tbsp.
- Chili, one tsp.
- Water, 200ml
- Shallots, half cup
- Carrots, one cup
- Cooked brown rice, four cups

Instructions:

1. Add the shallots and carrots with a pinch of salt and fry for ten minutes over a medium heat until softened and begin to caramelize.

2. Add coconut milk into the mixture.

3. Season and stir through half of the coriander and corn.

4. Spoon the curry into deep bowls, scatter with the remaining coriander and serve with rice and lime wedges for squeezing over.

7.4 Vegetarian Pad Thai Recipe

Cooking Time: 15 minutes

Serving Size: 4

Ingredients:

- Chopped green onions, three
- Fresh bean sprouts, half cup
- Garlic cloves, three
- Oil, three tbsp.

- Limes, two
- Red bell pepper, one
- Flat rice noodles, eight ounces
- Dry roasted peanuts, two cups
- Soy sauce, one tbsp.
- Light brown sugar, five tbsp.
- Fish sauce, three tbsp.
- Creamy peanut butter, two tbsp.
- Rice vinegar, two tbsp.
- Sirarcha hot sauce, one tbsp.

Instructions:

1. Cook noodles according to package instructions, just until tender.
2. Rinse under cold water.
3. Mix the sauce ingredients together. Add garlic and bell pepper in a wok.
4. Push everything to the side of the pan.
5. Add noodles, sauce, bean sprouts and peanuts to the pan.
6. Toss everything to combine.
7. Top with green onions, extra peanuts, cilantro and lime wedges.
8. Your dish is ready to be served.

7.5 Thai Vegetarian Red Curry Recipe

Cooking Time: 40 minutes

Serving Size: 4

Ingredients:

- Salt, a pinch
- Red bell pepper, one
- Coconut milk, one cup
- Red bell pepper, one
- Thai red curry paste, four tbsp.
- Butternut squash, one
- Vegetable oil, two tbsp.
- Chili, one tsp.
- Water, 200ml
- Shallots, half cup
- Brown rice cooked, four cups

Instructions:

1. Add the shallots with a pinch of salt and fry for ten minutes over a medium heat until softened and begin to caramelize.

2. Add the red curry paste and chili to the dish and fry for two minutes.

3. Tip in the squash and pepper, and then stir through the coconut milk along with 200ml water.

4. Season and stir through half the coriander. Spoon the curry into deep bowls, scatter with the remaining coriander and serve with rice and lime wedges for squeezing over.

7.6 Thai Vegetarian Fried Rice with Cashews Recipe

Cooking Time: 30 minutes

Serving Size: 4

Ingredients:

- Fish sauce, two tbsp.
- Soy sauce, half cup
- Cooked brown jasmine rice, three cups
- Tomatoes, two
- Cilantro, half cup
- Salt and pepper, to taste
- Vegetable oil, two tbsp.
- Thai chili peppers, three
- Toasted walnuts, half cup
- Onion, one
- Scallions, half cup
- Roasted cashews, half cup
- Minced garlic, one tsp.

Instructions:

1. Heat a large nonstick wok over high heat.
2. When the wok is very hot, add two tsp. of oil.
3. Add the remaining oil to the wok and add the onion, scallions and garlic.
4. Sauté for a minute, add the chili pepper if using, tomatoes and stir in all the rice.

5. Add the soy sauce and fish sauce. Stir to mix all the ingredients.

6. Keep stirring a few minutes and then add cashews on top.

7. Your dish is ready to be served.

7.7 Thai Vegetarian Noodles Recipe

Cooking Time: 25 minutes

Serving Size: 3

Ingredients:

- Coleslaw mix, one bag
- Green onions, a quarter cup
- Shredded carrots, half cup
- Honey roasted peanuts, half cup
- Oil, three tbsp.
- Linguini noodles, five ounces
- Cilantro, a quarter cup
- Soy sauce, one tbsp.
- Honey, five tbsp.
- Sesame oil, three tbsp.
- Red chili flakes, two tbsp.
- Minced garlic, four

Instructions:

1. Cook noodles. While noodles are being cooked, whisk together in a small bowl the soy sauce, honey, sesame oil, garlic and red pepper flakes.

2. Pour sauce onto drained noodles, and toss together.

3. Add shredded cabbage, shredded carrots and shredded cilantro to noodle mixture and mix.

4. Then gently stir in half of chopped cilantro, green onions and peanuts, reserving the other half for garnish.

5. Your dish is ready to be served.

7.8 Thai Vegetarian Kebabs Recipe

Cooking Time: 10 minutes

Serving Size: 4

Ingredients:

- Eggplant, one
- Pineapple, one can
- Tofu, two ounces
- Wooden skewers
- Maple syrup, one tbsp.
- Peanut butter, half cup
- Thai red curry paste, two tbsp.
- Rice vinegar, one tsp.
- Soy sauce, two tbsp.
- Garlic and ginger paste, one tsp.

Instructions:

1. Whisk together all of the marinade ingredients.

2. Cut the squash, pineapple and eggplant, and divide the pieces into eight equal piles. Cut the tofu and add the pieces to the piles.

3. Place the squash, pineapple and eggplant and tofu on the skewers, alternating as you go.

4. Lay the assembled kebabs on a cutting board or baking sheet, and brush with some of the marinade.

5. Grill on medium-high, or broil on high on a baking sheet or broiler pan, for about five minutes per side, or until the squash is tender.

6. Your kebabs are ready to be served.

7.9 Thai Vegetarian Soup Recipe

Cooking Time: 20 minutes

Serving Size: 4

Ingredients:

- Sliced mushrooms, one cup
- Vegetable stock, four cups
- Broccoli florets, three cups
- Coconut milk, a quarter cup
- Brown sugar, one tbsp.
- Soy sauce, one tsp.
- Thai green curry paste, two tbsp.
- Sesame oil, two tbsp.
- Salt to taste
- Crushed peanuts, one tbsp.
- Spring onion greens, one tbsp.
- Rice noodles, half pound
- Fresh basil, half cup

- Lime, two
- Minced garlic, one tsp.

Instructions:

1. Mix all the ingredients together and let it simmer for one hour.
2. Your soup is ready to be served.

7.10 Thai Yellow Curry Recipe

Cooking Time: 40 minutes

Serving Size: 4

Ingredients:

- Salt, a pinch
- Red bell pepper, one
- Coconut milk, one cup
- Red bell pepper, one
- Butternut squash, one
- Vegetable oil, two tbsp.
- Water, 200ml
- Shallots, half cup
- Brown rice, four

Instructions:

1. Add the shallots with a pinch of salt and fry for ten minutes over a medium heat until softened.
2. Tip in the squash and pepper, and then stir through the coconut milk along with 200ml water.
3. Season and stir through half of the coriander. Spoon the curry into deep bowls, scatter with the remaining

coriander and serve with rice and lime wedges for squeezing over.

7.11 Thai Tofu Green Curry Recipe

Cooking Time: 40 minutes

Serving Size: 4

Ingredients:

- Corn, half cup
- Salt, a pinch
- Coconut milk, one cup
- Thai green curry paste, four tbsp.
- Vegetable oil, two tbsp.
- Chili, one tsp.
- Tofu, two cups
- Water, 200ml
- Shallots, half cup
- Brown rice, four

Instructions:

1. Add the shallots with a pinch of salt and fry for ten mins over a medium heat until softened and begin to caramelize.

2. Add the curry paste and chili to the dish and fry for two minutes.

3. Tip in the tofu, and then stir through the coconut milk along with 200ml water.

4. Season and stir through half of the coriander and corn. Spoon the curry into deep bowls, scatter with the

remaining coriander and serve with rice and lime wedges for squeezing over.

7.12 Thai Tofu Green Curry with Quinoa Recipe

Cooking Time: 40 minutes

Serving Size: 4

Ingredients:

- Quinoa, four cups
- Salt, a pinch
- Coconut milk, one cup
- Thai green curry paste, four tbsp.
- Vegetable oil, two tbsp.
- Chili, one tsp.
- Tofu, two cups
- Water, 200ml
- Shallots, half cup

Instructions:

1. Add the shallots with a pinch of salt and fry for ten minutes over a medium heat until softened and begin to caramelize.

2. Add the curry paste and chili to the dish and fry for two mins.

3. Tip in the tofu, and then stir through the coconut milk along with 200ml water.

4. Season and stir through half of the coriander and corn. Spoon the curry into deep bowls, scatter with the remaining coriander and serve with cooked quinoa and lime wedges for squeezing over.

7.13 Thai Vegan Drunken Noodles Recipe

Cooking Time: 15 minutes

Serving Size: 2

Ingredients:

- Green onion, one
- Bell pepper, one
- Thai basil, a handful
- Garlic and ginger paste, one tsp.
- Sesame oil, two tbsp.
- Soy sauce, one tsp.
- Oyster sauce, one tsp.
- Fish sauce, one tsp.
- Salt and black pepper, to taste
- Red Thai chili, one
- Shallots, half cup

Instructions:

1. Cook the vegetables in the sesame oil.
2. Add spices and sauces into the mixture and then add the noodles and mix thoroughly.
3. Your dish is ready to be served.

7.14 Thai Pumpkin and Veggie Curry Recipe

Cooking Time: 40 minutes

Serving Size: 4

Ingredients:

- Corn, half cup
- Red bell pepper, two
- Pumpkin, two
- Salt, a pinch
- Coconut milk, one cup
- Thai red curry paste, four tbsp.
- Vegetable oil, two tbsp.
- Chili, one tsp.
- Butternut squash, two cups
- Water, 200ml
- Shallots, half cup
- Brown rice, four cups

Instructions:

1. Add the shallots with a pinch of salt and fry for ten minutes over a medium heat until softened.

2. Add the curry paste and chili to the dish and fry for two mins.

3. Tip in the pumpkin, vegetables, and then stir through the coconut milk along with 200ml water.

4. Season and stir through half of the coriander and corn. Spoon the curry into deep bowls, scatter with the

remaining coriander and serve with rice and lime wedges for squeezing over.

7.15 Thai Veggie Burger Recipe

Cooking Time: 10 minutes

Serving Size: 4

Ingredients:

- Thai red curry paste, two tbsp.
- Salt, a pinch
- Mix vegetables, two cups
- Thai red curry paste, four tbsp.
- Vegetable oil, two tbsp.
- Green onions, half cup
- Cilantro, half cup
- Garlic and ginger paste, one tsp.
- Thai pickles, as required
- Bread buns, four

Instructions:

1. Mix all the stuff for the burger mixture together and make patty.
2. Fry the patties and then assemble the patty burger by adding pickles into it.
3. Your burger is ready to be served.

7.16 Thai Vegetarian Quinoa Chili Recipe

Cooking Time: 120 minutes

Serving Size: 6-8

Ingredients:

- Quinoa, two cups
- Coconut milk, half cup
- Vegetable broth, half cup
- Thai red curry paste, four tbsp.
- Olive oil, two tbsp.
- Green onions, half cup
- Chili powder, one tsp.
- Curry paste, one tbsp.
- Green bell pepper, one
- Sweet potato, one cup
- Tomatoes, one cup
- Salt and pepper, to taste
- Garlic and ginger paste, one tsp.
- Thai pickles, as required
- Greek yoghurt, as required

Instructions:

1. In a large Dutch oven or soup pot, whisk together the chili powder; curry paste, cumin and a few tablespoons of broth over medium-low heat until smooth.

2. Add in onion, green pepper, garlic, sweet potato and olive oil and sauté for five minutes or until veggies are tender.

3. Add in remaining broth, beans, quinoa, coconut milk, tomatoes, salt and pepper and bring to a boil.

4. Reduce to simmer and cook for about an hour, or until flavors are mixed and quinoa is cooked.

5. Serve topped with sliced green onions and plain Greek yogurt.

7.17 Thai Slow Cooker Vegetable Massaman Curry Recipe

Cooking Time: 3 hours

Serving Size: 6

Ingredients:

- Quinoa, two cups
- Coconut milk, half cup
- Vegetable broth, half cup
- Tomatoes, half cup
- Brown sugar, one tsp.
- Tamari sauce, one tbsp.
- Cauliflower, one
- Potato, one cup
- Green beans, one cup
- Salt and pepper, to taste
- Sirarcha hot sauce, one tsp.
- Peanut butter, half cup
- Peanuts, half cup

Instructions:

1. Stir in the broth, tomatoes, fish sauce, tamari and brown sugar.

2. Add the cauliflower and potatoes, and toss to coat. Cover and cook until the vegetables are tender.

3. Combine the coconut milk and peanut butter in a heatproof bowl and microwave until warm.

4. Pour the coconut milk mixture into the slow cooker, and add the green beans and peanuts. Cover and cook until warmed through.

5. Add the sriracha, and season with salt and pepper.

6. Serve the curry over rice or quinoa, and sprinkle with chopped peanuts and cilantro.

7.18 Thai Slow Cooker Yellow Curry Recipe

Cooking Time: 2 hours

Serving Size: 4

Ingredients:

- Salt, a pinch
- Chickpeas, two cups
- Coconut milk, one cup
- Butternut squash, one
- Vegetable oil, two tbsp.
- Water, 500ml
- Carrots, two cups
- Brown rice, four cups

Instructions:

1. Tip in the chickpeas, butternut squash and carrots. Then stir through the coconut milk along with 500ml water.

2. Season and stir through half of the coriander.

3. Spoon the curry into deep bowls, scatter with the remaining coriander and serve with rice and lime wedges for squeezing over.

7.19 Thai Slow Cooker Pineapple Vegetarian Curry Recipe

Cooking Time: 2 hours

Serving Size: 4

Ingredients:

- Salt, a pinch
- Pineapple, two cups
- Coconut milk, one cup
- Mix vegetables, one cup
- Vegetable oil, two tbsp.
- Water, 200ml
- Curry powder, two tsp.
- Crushed red pepper, one tbsp.
- Minced garlic, half tsp.
- Brown rice, four cups

Instructions:

1. Whisk together the coconut milk, curry powder, salt, crushed red pepper and garlic in a slow cooker.

2. Add the remaining ingredients and cook for two hours.

3. Your dish is ready to be served with brown rice or jasmine rice.

7.20 Thai Slow Cooker Vegetable and Tofu Stew Recipe

Cooking Time: 3 hours

Serving Size: 4

Ingredients:

- Salt, a pinch
- Tofu, two cups
- Coconut milk, one cup
- Mix vegetables, one cup
- Vegetable oil, two tbsp.
- Water, 200ml
- Crushed red pepper, one tbsp.
- Minced garlic, half tsp.
- Curry powder, two tsp.

Instructions:

Whisk together the coconut milk, curry powder, salt, crushed red pepper and garlic in a slow cooker.

1. Add the remaining ingredients and cook for three hours.

2. Your dish is ready to be served with brown rice or jasmine rice.

7.21 Thai Slow Cooker Potato Soup Recipe

Cooking Time: 120 minutes

Serving Size: 2

Ingredients:

- Potato, three cups
- Garlic cloves, four
- Water, four cups
- Coriander seeds, two teaspoons
- Chopped coriander, a handful
- Hot paprika, two tsp.
- Grated lemon zest, two
- Kaffir lime leaves, four
- Coconut milk, one cup

Instructions:

1. Mix all the ingredients together and cover it to simmer for two hours.
2. Your soup is ready to be served.

7.22 Thai Slow Cooker Green Tofu Soup Recipe

Cooking Time: 120 minutes

Serving Size: 3

Ingredients:

- Tofu, three cups
- Garlic cloves, four
- Water, four cups

- Thai green curry paste, two tbsp.
- Coriander seeds, two teaspoons
- Chopped coriander, a handful
- Hot paprika, two tsp.
- Grated lemon zest, two
- Kaffir lime leaves, four
- Coconut milk, one cup

Instructions:

1. Mix all the ingredients together and cover it to simmer for two hours.
2. Your soup is ready to be served.

7.23 Thai Slow Cooker Eggplant Curry Recipe

Cooking Time: 3 hours

Serving Size: 4

Ingredients:

- Salt, a pinch
- Eggplant, two cups
- Coconut milk, one cup
- Cilantro, one cup
- Vegetable oil, two tbsp.
- Water, 500ml
- Crushed red pepper, one tbsp.
- Minced garlic, half tsp.
- Curry powder, two tsp.

- Brown or jasmine rice, two cups

Instructions:

1. Whisk together the coconut milk, curry powder, salt, crushed red pepper and garlic in a slow cooker.

2. Add the remaining ingredients and cook for three hours.

3. Your dish is ready to be served with brown rice or jasmine rice.

7.24 Thai Slow Cooker Chicken Curry Recipe

Cooking Time: 3 hours

Serving Size: 4

Ingredients:

- Salt, a pinch
- Chicken breast pieces, two pounds
- Coconut milk, one cup
- Cilantro, one cup
- Vegetable oil, two tbsp.
- Water, 500ml
- Crushed red pepper, one tbsp.
- Minced garlic, half tsp.
- Curry powder, two tsp.
- Brown or jasmine rice, two cups

Instructions:

1. Whisk together the coconut milk, curry powder, salt, crushed red pepper and garlic in a slow cooker.

2. Add the remaining ingredients and cook for three hours.

3. Your dish is ready to be served with brown rice or jasmine rice.

7.25 Thai Slow Cooker Pumpkin Soup Recipe

Cooking Time: 2 hours

Serving Size: 4

Ingredients:

- Corn, half cup
- Pumpkin, two cups
- Salt, a pinch
- Coconut milk, one cup
- Thai red curry paste, four tbsp.
- Vegetable oil, two tbsp.
- Chili, one tsp.
- Water, 500ml

Instructions:

1. Add the curry paste and chili to the dish and fry for two mins.

2. Tip in the pumpkin, and then stir through the coconut milk along with 500ml water.

3. Season and stir through half of the coriander and corn.

4. Your soup is ready to be served.

7.26 Thai Slow Cooker Peanut Chicken Curry Recipe

Cooking Time: 3 hours

Serving Size: 4

Ingredients:

- Salt, a pinch
- Chicken breast pieces, two pounds
- Coconut milk, one cup
- Cilantro, one cup
- Vegetable oil, two tbsp.
- Water, 200ml
- Peanuts, half cup
- Crushed red pepper, one tbsp.
- Minced garlic, half tsp.
- Curry powder, two tsp.
- Brown or jasmine rice, two cups

Instructions:

1. Whisk together the coconut milk, curry powder, salt, crushed red pepper and garlic in a slow cooker.

2. Add the remaining ingredients and cook for three hours.

3. Your dish is ready to be served with brown rice or jasmine rice.

7.27 Thai Slow Cooker Beef Curry Recipe

Cooking Time: 4 hours

Serving Size: 4

Ingredients:

- Salt, a pinch
- Beef pieces, two pounds
- Coconut milk, one cup
- Cilantro, one cup
- Vegetable oil, two tbsp.
- Water, 500ml
- Crushed red pepper, one tbsp.
- Minced garlic, half tsp.
- Curry powder, two tsp.
- Brown or jasmine rice, two cups

Instructions:

1. Whisk together the coconut milk, curry powder, salt, crushed red pepper and garlic in a slow cooker.
2. Add the remaining ingredients and cook for four hours.
3. Your dish is ready to be served with brown rice or jasmine rice.

7.28 Thai Slow Cooker Coconut Curry Lentils Recipe

Cooking Time: 4 hours

Serving Size: 4

Ingredients:

- Salt, a pinch
- Brown lentils, two cups
- Coconut milk, one cup
- Carrots, one cup
- Tomatoes, two cups
- Cilantro, one cup
- Vegetable oil, two tbsp.
- Water, 500ml
- Crushed red pepper, one tbsp.
- Minced garlic, half tsp.
- Curry powder, two tsp.
- Brown or jasmine rice, two cups

Instructions:

1. Whisk together the coconut milk, curry powder, salt, crushed red pepper and garlic in a slow cooker.
2. Add the remaining ingredients and cook for four hours.
3. Your dish is ready to be served with brown rice or jasmine rice.

7.29 Thai Slow Cooker Chicken Carrot Potato Soup Recipe

Cooking Time: 3 hours

Serving Size: 4

Ingredients:

- Potato, three cups

- Garlic cloves, four
- Water, four cups
- Carrots, three cups
- Chicken, two pounds
- Coriander seeds, two teaspoons
- Chopped coriander, a handful
- Hot paprika, two tsp.
- Grated lemon zest, two
- Kaffir lime leaves, four
- Coconut milk, one cup

Instructions:

1. Mix all the ingredients together and cover it to simmer for three hours.
2. Your soup is ready to be served.

7.30 Thai Slow Cooker Butternut Squash Soup Recipe

Cooking Time: 3 hours

Serving Size: 4

Ingredients:

- Butternut Squash, three cups
- Garlic cloves, four
- Water, four cups
- Coriander seeds, two teaspoons
- Chopped coriander, a handful
- Hot paprika, two tsp.

- Grated lemon zest, two
- Kaffir lime leaves, four
- Coconut milk, one cup

Instructions:

1. Mix all the ingredients together and cover it to simmer for three hours.

2. Your soup is ready to be served.

7.31 Thai Slow Cooker Coconut Quinoa Curry Recipe

Cooking Time: 3 hours

Serving Size: 4

Ingredients:

- Salt, a pinch
- Coconut milk, one cup
- Cilantro, one cup
- Vegetable oil, two tbsp.
- Water, 500ml
- Crushed red pepper, one tbsp.
- Minced garlic, half tsp.
- Curry powder, two tsp.
- Quinoa, two cups

Instructions:

1. Whisk together the coconut milk, curry powder, salt, crushed red pepper and garlic in a slow cooker.

2. Add the remaining ingredients and cook for three hours.

3. Your dish is ready to be served.

7.32 Thai Slow Cooker Whole Cauliflower Curry Recipe

Cooking Time: 3 hours

Serving Size: 4

Ingredients:

- Salt, a pinch
- Coconut milk, one cup
- Cilantro, one cup
- Cauliflower, one whole
- Vegetable oil, two tbsp.
- Water, 500ml
- Crushed red pepper, one tbsp.
- Minced garlic, half tsp.
- Curry powder, two tsp.
- Quinoa, two cups

Instructions:

1. Whisk together the coconut milk, curry powder, salt, crushed red pepper and garlic in a slow cooker.

2. Add the remaining ingredients and cook for three hours.

3. Your dish is ready to be served with any rice of your choice.

7.33 Thai Slow Cooker Salmon Curry Recipe

Cooking Time: 2 hours

Serving Size: 4

Ingredients:

- Salt, a pinch
- Salmon filet pieces, two pounds
- Coconut milk, one cup
- Cilantro, one cup
- Vegetable oil, two tbsp.
- Water, 500ml
- Crushed red pepper, one tbsp.
- Minced garlic, half tsp.
- Curry powder, two tsp.
- Brown or jasmine rice, two cups

Instructions:

1. Whisk together the coconut milk, curry powder, salt, crushed red pepper and garlic in a slow cooker.
2. Add the remaining ingredients and cook for two hours.
3. Your dish is ready to be served with brown rice or jasmine rice.

7.34 Thai Slow Cooker Chicken Pumpkin Curry Recipe

Cooking Time: 3 hours

Serving Size: 4

Ingredients:

- Salt, a pinch
- Chicken breast pieces, two pounds
- Coconut milk, one cup
- Cilantro, one cup
- Vegetable oil, two tbsp.
- Water, 500ml
- Pumpkin, two cups
- Crushed red pepper, one tbsp.
- Minced garlic, half tsp.
- Curry powder, two tsp.
- Brown or jasmine rice, two cups

Instructions:

1. Whisk together the coconut milk, curry powder, salt, crushed red pepper and garlic in a slow cooker.
2. Add the remaining ingredients and cook for three hours.
3. Your dish is ready to be served with brown rice or jasmine rice.

7.35 Thai Slow Cooker Noodles Soup Recipe

Cooking Time: 2 hours

Serving Size: 4

Ingredients:

- Rice noodles, three cups
- Garlic cloves, four

- Chicken broth, four cups
- Coriander seeds, two teaspoons
- Chopped coriander, a handful
- Hot paprika, two tsp.
- Grated lemon zest, two
- Kaffir lime leaves, four
- Coconut milk, one cup

Instructions:

1. Mix all the ingredients together and cover it to simmer for two hours.
2. Your soup is ready to be served.

All the recipes in this chapter are easy to make on your own.

Conclusion

While living a busy life food becomes the only source of happiness for individuals in the 21st century. Different cuisines are available in the world, each of them being totally different from the other. Thai cuisine covers dishes from Thailand and Thai foods are extremely popular in the U.S.A.

In this book, we have discussed different aspects of Thai cuisine along with the Thai recipes. We have discussed in detail the history and origin of Thai foods. Light was thrown upon the evolution of Thai foods over time and the reason behind the popularity of this cuisine in the U.S.A. We have also discussed the advantages of cooking Thai food at home rather than going out for meals or having it delivered to your door stop.

The various spices used in Thai cooking have enormous amount of amazing properties that can have a positive and healthy impact on our overall health. This cookbook includes 100+ recipes that contain breakfast, lunch, dinner, dessert, famous, alternative, as well as slow cooker and vegetarian recipes that you can easily make at home without supervision of any kind. So, why to order or go out for Thai food when you can be the chef at your home? Now make your family and loved ones crave for this delicious food.

Printed in Great Britain
by Amazon